Definition of An Ex-Wife

Definition of An Ex-Wife

The SURVIVAL Story

Athena Grace

NEWLEAF

Definition of an Ex-Wife by Athena Grace

ISBN 978-1-955136-94-5 (Paperback)

This book is written to provide information and motivation to readers. Its purpose is not to render any type of psychological, legal, or professional advice of any kind. The content is the sole opinion and expression of the author, and not necessarily that of the publisher.

Printed in the United States of America
New Leaf Media, LLC
175 S. 3rd Street, Ste 200
Columbus, OH 43215
www.thenewleafmedia.com

Dedication

As a wise man once suggested to me—yes a man—I should dedicate this book to every person (male and female) who has entered into the world of divorce willingly or unwillingly. You have a voice whether or not you know it, and the world does not stop just because your partner has gone into another realm. You can make it to the next step of your life; there is a plan for you.

Special Dedication

This book is dedicated to Mary, my co-worker, who has struggled with her impending divorce throughout my book and to this day. She is stronger than she knows, but she must devise a plan to get to the next point in her life. She can do it, and with the help of her friends, she can tell that "bastard" to get out of her life for good.

Table of Contents

Acknowledgements

Several people mentioned in my book are friends, co-workers, and acquaintances. Thank you for allowing me to include your account along the "divorce trail," along with my own. I feel we are in the same boat, but we are not all sinking together. Our strength lies within us all, so we can survive to the next phase of our existence.

My own experiences listed in this book are ones that have inspired me, and some have even made me physically ill. However, they have all one thing in common, I have gotten much of my strength from this knowledge that they have provided. They are my source of comfort and my source of therapy. Everyone going through a divorce is currently at a different level of coping; we can learn from one another's suffering and pain. Life will go on, but on a different platform than before. There is a life we were meant for, and it will comfort us once again; thereby, the pain of divorce will be lessened.

CHAPTER I –

The Saga Begins

A marriage can be such a fragile thing, but it can also be one of the best relationships two people can have. In my case it wasn't so; our vows, "to death due us part," was the beginning of the end for us. My story is not the first and will not be the last when it comes to divorce. I have just expressed my emotions through words that may help others, both men and women, through one of the most difficult times of one's life. This is my true story of coping with tragedy and my ultimate survival.

For months, or maybe over a year, things weren't right in our relationship. We had been together for almost 19 years, and things were changing more dramatically the last few months.

His overnight poker games, and the classes he would take on Thursday nights started me wondering if he really was where he said. He would call later in the evening and say that he wouldn't be home because he was going drinking with his buddies after his class. This started a flickering little light in my brain that I couldn't shake nor could I turn it off. He would also leave really early on Saturday and Sunday mornings and wouldn't be home for hours— well after dinnertime. Even my neighbors began to notice that his truck was never here. The staleness in our relationship was getting more pronounced. Our last anniversary he had forgotten, and there were no flowers on Valentine's Day. Was it that we had been together for so long that we were now taking advantage of each other? I mean, a couple of years ago, I forgot our anniversary, and felt terrible about it. Now, he had no desire to kiss nor hug me anymore either, and after two years of being in a relationship without intimacy, I got distant too. I even moved out of the Master Bedroom. At first it was due to a car accident that hurt my lower back, and I couldn't stand the mattress because it was too hard. But, after a while, I really enjoyed not sleeping in the same room with him. His loud snoring, the way he took over the bed, and his constant allergy attacks irritated me. I knew our relationship was in trouble, so maybe part of his ultimate actions were my fault. Because he never wanted to touch me anymore, I just knew he was getting his affection somewhere else; but with who? Maybe

I didn't care. Maybe I didn't want to be with him anymore and we were just going through the motions of man and wife—you know, paying bills, taking care of our son, etc. But it seemed that I took over a lot of the household duties more than him. For, he never did laundry, vacuuming, dusting, dishes, ironing. You name it; he DIDN'T do it. Maybe I put forth too much effort when we were dating. For it seemed that I did too many household chores and he got used to it. I mean, he really was a slob, and "a slob is a slob is a slob," right? Well, it was for him, and I put up with it. So, blame me as much as him for not having an equal relationship. I guess I realized it was over, but I didn't know how to gain back my strength to proceed onward. However, through prayer, I was finally at my wits-end and found the courage and the timing to do what was necessary.

It was June 20, 2009; it just one day before Father's Day and our son and his grandmother planned a vacation to Texas to see relatives. My husband had taken our son to breakfast and then he proceeded to take them both to the airport. I had plans to run errands that morning and then go to a movie in the afternoon. The morning had gotten away from me, and now I found myself at the movie theatre. I had just gotten settled in my seat, and my son called me to say he had arrived at his destination. I told him that I was in the movie theatre and that the movie was about to begin, but that I'd call him upon the conclusion. After just a few hours, I left the theatre and proceeded to call back my son. My sister-in-law answered and informed me that he was on the other phone with his dad and would return my call after he finished. Just a few minutes had passed, there was my son calling to tell me how excited he was to be in Texas. I told him that his aunt had just told me that he had finished a call from his dad. Now was my time to put my plan into action. I asked him, "So, where's your dad?" He replied with, "He's at work." Well, sometimes this was true on a Saturday and sometimes even on a Sunday; today I didn't believe it. So, I proceeded to his office, which just happened to be just down the street from where I was going. I drove passed the parking lot, but didn't see his truck. I turned around and proceeded back, pulled into the parking lot, and then I drove behind the building. My gut feeling had to be right! He was lying again; I just knew it! I'm not sure what my emotions were, but I almost wimped out and went home. I got half way home, and had a judgment call, so I turned around. I had a gut feeling who she was, and I just happened to know where she lived. She was just 10 minutes away, so I proceeded to his office, which so happened to be just down the street. At this point, my heartwas pounding faster than ever. Would I be wrong? I've felt that way before. I mean, my heart was telling me one thing and my head was telling me another. Did he really have it in him to cheat on me? Many questions raced through my mind in the 10 minute drive there. As I turned into her housing development, and mad the first right—there, the third house on the right was his truck parked in her driveway. The garage door was open and a lawn mover was in sight, but he was nowhere to be found. I slowly drove passed, but didn't see anyone, not even her. I drove to the end of the cul-de-sac, turned around, and drove right passed her house again. There again, no one was out front. At that moment, my heart was racing even faster and my hands were shaking as if to be nervous. I knew I couldn't stop or I would have done something I would have regretted. All the way home, I think I was in shock. What was my plan now? I was pretty sure I had found out my answer, but I didn't know for sure. Was he just there helping her with some domestic chore? If the answer were "yes," then why would he lie to his son about his location? Well, they had been friends for a long time, so it may have just been innocent and I was jumping to conclusions.

I even thought she was my friend. But today was different. Today, I had to have answers, but I didn't know how to proceed. What would I say and when would I get a chance to say it? I got home and various scenarios went streaming through my mind. Before I knew it, 30 minutes had past, and I was ajar from my thoughts as the phone rang. It was him telling me that he wouldn't be home tonight for there, again, was another poker party with the guys. There it was, another lie, I just knew it. I'm not sure what gave me the strength to ask, but the words just flowed out. "So, did she get her grass mowed?" I asked. His reply was, "Well I guess so." I then asked, "Do you want to live with her?" He replied, "I would like too!" Right then, my heart just sank. All of my suspicions about his actions, and thinking I was going crazy, suddenly flooded my brain—he was cheating, and all this time hewanted to be with "her!" My next comment was, "So, when can you come get your stuff?" He replied, "Tomorrow." My next remark was that I had thought something like this was going on for a while, and he said, smugly, "Well, I wanted our son to get help with his medical issue first." I then proceed to tell him that I would file the paperwork within the next day or so. He agreed. There, in a flash of less than 5 minutes, my marriage of almost 19 years was dead! I hung up the phone and I can't remember my first reaction, but I immediately starting calling my girlfriends.

I couldn't breath, but I know the tears were falling too fast for me to think anymore. I guess I knew what was going on, but I was devastated with the truth, and it wasn't me who left for another man. This marriage wasn't working, but did he have to do this to me? Now lying on the table was all of the lies, all of the deceit—was I not worth him just leaving me, and not into another woman's arms all within 24 hours? I didn't know the answers, but I had to talk to someone. So, I started dialing. Everyone I could think of flooded my brain. Most of them, however, were not answering their phones; however, I did get in touch with his sister, and asked her to remove herself from my son's presence so he would not hear any of this mess. Was she surprised? Who knows? I told her what her brother had done to me, and that I was filing for divorce. There, the word camc out—ouch! Maybe it wasn't something she was crazy about for she, too, went through a divorce just a year prior. It was she who wanted out of a marriage with a verbally abusive man who couldn't care for himself, but it does take two to tangle. So, who knows what else happened in her relationship that matched mine. But at this moment, it was my time to fall apart, and I needed a close friend to be with me. After a few more calls I did get in touch with a close co-worker who came to my rescue. Within 20 minutes she was there on my doorstep to listen to my ills. By the time she pulled up, my eyes had filled with tears once again and they were red with pain. She didn't really initially hear what had happened due to my shaky voice, but she listened once again to my afternoon saga. We then went inside and sat at the table. At that point, I knew it was so true. All of the questions that were running through my mind had now been answered. All of the nights he said he was with the guys, at a class or where ever, he must have been with her! He needed an excuse to be with her over night, and that was his out. Was I devastated? I don't know. Did I care? Even that question was fuzzy. The only thing I knew was that he needed

7

to get out of my life with the word "spouse" attached to it. So, after my co-worker consoled me for several hours, and watched me down almost a whole bottle of wine, I told her I was ok, and now needed to precede packing up his things. I accumulated several boxes and trash bags and then stuffed as much as I could into each container. By the time I was too tired to think, I had removed all of his clothes and shoes from the closet to include knickknacks and all of his toiletries. I was on a mission to get rid of him and his possessions. I then proceeded downstairs to remove pictures that were his and his favorite glasses. Did the thought occur to me to break everything that should go to him? Of course it did, but I struggled through my ordeal with dignity. I'm not sure how or why, but I did it. I even found some newspaper to wrap them in—was I being too nice? Probably. But, part of me just wanted him gone for good and I was trying to push my emotions aside. An angel must have been watching and guiding me through these minutes and hours, for I don't know why I did what I did—and with self-esteem. I had no inkling to destroy any of his possessions. Why? I don't know why—but, maybe it was due to the fact that I am in my mid-40s and perhaps had a new outlook on a situation that would have probably destroyed me if I was in my 20s.

It was <u>Day 2,</u> and of all days it was Father's Day. He was coming over to get his things and leave permanently. I didn't know when he was coming—only that he was coming. I didn't sleep much that night—perhaps an hour or so. My face was puffy, my eyes were red, and I was exhausted from sleep deprivation. It must have been 1 p.m. or so, and I thought I had heard a noise in the garage. I got up from the couch, and proceeded though the door that led to the garage. I could see the garage door was open, and there to my right he was standing. Just a few steps, and I was right beside him. He looked quite distraught, but ready for a fight. As I opened my mouth to say something, it was as if he thought I was going to yell at him for his adulteress actions. He was very surprised to find that I said I wanted this situation to be amicable. I don't think I had ever seen him so humbled. Was it the fact that I busted him before he could surprise me? Maybe. Or was it the fact that I caught him off guard with the biggest lie he ever told me, and for the first time in our relationship; he didn't know how to handle it? There were times where I could get him speechless, but it didn't happen very often. He was always pretty good about having the perfect "come back" line, but not today. I even informed him that I had packed up most of his things, and had inventoried the whole house. I had gotten organized, and I don't know how I had the strength to do it so quickly. It seemed like he was there for hours getting his things, but the actual time was much less. He had made three trips—the last one with a buddy who had a truck. I was very surprised to find that he didn't want many things. He didn't take any furniture, only the necessities. Well, duh? She already had everything—I guess I didn't think about it at that time, but it did hit me later. Maybe I just wanted him to get the things that irritated me about him out of the house. All of his tools, that stupid deer head he had on the wall in the Master Bedroom, and his gun cabinet—also in the Master Bedroom. Who puts things like that in a Master Bedroom? Only a "Bachelor Want A Be" I guess. But, now they were going away for good. Over to her house—Hah! Does she know what she's getting? How could another woman do this to her "lover's" wife? Doesn't she know that karma could come back to bite her? I mean, really, how could someone literally put a knife into another person's back like that? All of the hateful, cruel things in life have ended up in my lap, because of their wants and desires. No one asked me if I wanted this, and no one asked our son or her daughters. The word "selfishness" seemed to stream though my blood at this point and it started to boil. I had so many emotions: I didn't know which one of them to choose to deal with first.

<u>Day 3</u> – It was Monday, and my head was still a wreck, but I wanted to file for divorce and get the clock running. Because, by the 91 st day, I could be single again and my "anchor of almost 19 years" could be gone—at least from my home. But, alas, he asked to cancel today and meet tomorrow—for what reason I still don't know. Can you say, "Control Freak"? Here we go again; another day he has control over me, and I despised him once again. Well, I had other plans. I went over to the courthouse and inquired about how I should proceed. I had some questions on filing and whether I needed to file for dissolution of divorce or for a legal separation. I didn't know if you had to do one then the other—this was all foreign to me. I mean the minister doesn't give you this training in marriage counseling before you say your, "I do's." She stated that I could do one or the other. You don't have to be legally separated and then get a divorce. I told her that I wanted him gone since he cheated on me. Her face said it

all—she had heard this one before, and shyly lowered her head.

Well, I got my solution. If I file for separation, it would take longer, and divorce seemed something that wouldn't take as much time. There was my answer; I wanted rid of him—that chick can have him, and I wanted it final! Don't get me wrong, I'm not a normally vindictive person. But if someone stabs me in the back in this way, I'm done with them, once and for all. I really don't have a problem getting rid of a relationship in my life that is not supportive of me, and me of them. I can be the most faithful person in the world, but really—why someone puts up with a person who doesn't respect you is not worth having in your life. Well, here's another 24 hours I need to wait to begin my new life; figures…

Day 4 – It was 9 a.m. Tuesday morning, and he said that he would meet me at my office. So, I waited at the front reception area for him. By 9:15 a.m., I went back to my desk and there was a phone message from him asking if it was ok for him to come now. Well, what part of 9 a.m. didn't he get? It just seemed like another control issue that he was using. Well, I called him and said to come over now. Well, about 10 minutes later he finally showed up. So, I went out into the hallway to meet him. We then proceeded upstairs to get some paperwork notarized.

One of the first things out of his mouth was that he wasn't going to pay maintenance to me;even though he was once the "bread winner" of the family. That arrogant asshole! First, he cheats on me, and then he thinks he didn't do anything wrong, and that he shouldn't make any amends! I think my face was red with anger and I could feel my muscles tensing up. But, I kept my wits about me. I'm glad, because he then said he would pay me a substantial amount per month for child support even though we would have joint custody. Ok, that would work too since I never got that much out of him before, so I thought I'd take it and run. My hesitancy of trying to make amends was rescinded, and we then proceeded to finish the paperwork.

This whole scenario got me to thinking. I guess the process of attempting a life change—financially and then ending a long relationship, has different effects on people. For example, this man had been riding so high at one point in his life—you know the type, making a lot of money, constant appreciation by his clients, and also by his business contacts. Then, thinking he would never get caught doing something he shouldn't have done. I think he finally had some guilt, or even embarrassment—perhaps I'm wrong? He must have thought he was invincible or at least a god! Now, his job had changed, and he had to came to a realization that what he was once getting paid in one month, in the mortgage field, he was now making the same amount over a period of six months. Was it his ego that stumped him? Did he need someone else to make him feel better than I ever had?

Perhaps. Maybe it was he who had become someone who needed to be in a pair of bigger "britches" as we would say in the South. I didn't know any of these answers, but we needed to finish what we had started today.

He didn't know that I had gone to the courthouse yesterday. For, I didn't want him to once again, have the upper edge on me. Since he couldn't meet to file the paperwork on Monday, it worked out and I felt a sense of calm, if you can call it that. So, after the papers were notarized, we both proceeded over to the courthouse since it was only a block from my office. We drove in separate vehicles because I didn't or couldn't be that close to him—not today. We met in the front of the courthouse and walked in together, amicably, to my surprise. After going through security, we proceeded to the Clerk of the Court. We just so happened to get assistance from the same lady from my first visit yesterday.

As we both walked up to her, I commented that I remembered her from yesterday and that she was at the other window. She immediately said that she remembered me, and there again was that sheepish smile, for she knew what he had done, but she kept her mouth shut. I think she was surprised that we had arrived together to file. I'm sure that most of the time, there are more tears and grief-stricken stories she's heard than plain talk and civil obedience. I guess it didn't matter, for we both handed her our initial paperwork, and she recorded it as we paid our fee. There it was—my hard-earned money had to be spent on another one of "his" decisions! I guess the only good thing about it was that I had the money. Of course, he had to put it on a credit card— his one and only way to pay for everything lately. At least I had that pulling for me. I could actually pay for this next adventure with a check from my checking account and not charge it. Hooray for me!!

After about 15 minutes, the clock started ticking. The 91st day would be upon us sooner than we thought. I felt somewhat relieved, but very unsure of what my future would bring. As we walked down the corridor, I asked him one last question that was still stuck in my mind. "If it were me who had cheated, would he be acting like I was now?" His immediate response was "yes." Seriously? That boy has lied so much in his life, he continues to drool lies from every word coming out of his mouth. Please, he would tell everyone and his banker that I was the "Ho" that did him wrong! He was lying through his teeth and he knew it! I didn't buy it for a second. Maybe I just wanted one "dig" of my own, and now it was done.

As we continued to chat, I now noticed the front door wasn't very far away. As we proceeded outside, we continued to talk. I guess mostly about our son and how we would handle the situation when he came back home from his vacation with grandma. We

15

stood close to where I parked and talked for at least the next 40 minutes. He kept talking about our son and how he wanted to put him first in this situation. My thoughts went the other direction because he had never put our son first in anything—especially in this situation. He was only thinking of himself, and what he wanted. The only person who was first in his life was the person he saw in the mirror. It was me who cared for our son since infancy. I remember a time when he was first born and we went out to a restaurant. I was getting our son out of the car, and he proceeded to get out, close the car door and was heading down the sidewalk to the restaurant. As he turned around to see where I was, his response was "oh." He had forgotten our son—how do you forget an infant in a car? That's how selfish he was, and he didn't change in the 13 years since our son was born. It was me who changed diapers, fed him, clothed him, and there when he was sick.

My soon-to-be ex was such a solitary man; in that I mean he cared only for his own needs. Other people's needs were secondary. For example, I remember a time when I had strep throat, and I was doing laundry. He told me that maybe I should lie down and rest. I told him that the laundry wouldn't get done by itself. His response was, "You can do it later." He didn't even offer to help with that chore. Why the hell I didn't leave then, I'll never know. I truly believe all of these years of torment led us to this day—our day of reckoning. I mean, I could count on one hand how many diapers he changed in the years of "diaper management" training for new parents, and he was proud of that fact! It was quite the effort to even ask him to pick up our son from daycare, for there was always an excuse why he couldn't. It was he who had put himself first in every situation. It was only this year—the year our son turned 13—when he finally stepped up to the plate. He was now spending more time with him as "father and son." Then, he started paying for some necessary medical treatments—Oh My God, what happened? Maybe he had to vindicate himself into believing that he really was a good dad? How could a parent think you can be absent for "umpteen" years and then make up for this inactivity in just six months? He had to either be stoned or drunk, but in his case, his new chick must have given him the encouragement.

Day 5 –Today is Wednesday. I can't believe it's the fifth day after my initial melt down, and starting today he's out of town. It's a business trip for his boss or something—or so he says. I'm having a hard time believing anything he says from now on. Besides, does the new chick believe that's where he went? I still wonder how you can start a new relationship based on lies and deceit! No matter what happens from now on, I don't want him back. She can have him now, and I guess the sad part is that I know her. I've even been to her house! I don't know why, but I can't confront her yet—just her name makes me cringe. My next days, months, and years will be quite a challenge for me, so I have to proceed with caution in everything I now do.

Today I can't keep my thoughts straight. I am edgy. I can't sit or be in one place for any length of time. My stomach is still in knots; I don't even have an appetite since Day 1. Alcohol calms me some, and I so appreciate my friends who are there for me. My co-workers are astonished as to my dilemma, and I'm getting advice left and right on how to cope. Also, it seems as if everyone at work has a big dilemma in addition to me. Does crap happen all at once to everybody? As for me, I want to eat, but I resist—why bother? I have lost three pounds thus far and that was in the first three days. At least I now have a diet that works, but I wouldn't recommend it to anyone. I hate to admit it, but I now have something in common with a co-worker who left last year. She, too, went through the same thing recently and she has dropped at least 30-35 pounds. She looks great, but she also seems to have a wide variety of emotions to deal with—I now understand those emotions.

No one can ever prepare you for a divorce—it's like death that tugs at your emotional heartstrings. Maybe in a way they're both tied together. It's an emotional sensation that rips your heart out of your body, and no one can really put it back the way it was before. Besides, every female that I have known, who has gone through a divorce, has seemed to "survive," but what really were they going through and at what cost? How did they do it? What kept them alive to get through the next day? Did they have prayer in their life? I didn't know, but my real-life journey through the "D" word was just starting, and I was about to find out. I know now that my faith is stronger than it has ever been because of what I'm going through. My soon-to-be ex never really wanted to believe in God, even though he went to a Southern Baptist school where "church" was an everyday thing. Maybe he was burnt out after constantly reading the bible and studying the Word. All I know is that during this past year, his faith was tattered and torn to a point that he said he didn't believe in God anymore. All of this was gibberish and fake—it was just an excuse. He acted like religion was force-fed to him by a tube, and now he was ripping out the needle and throwing away every part of his belief into the garbage. If you ask me, I think he gave up the notion of a higher power a long time ago—not just 12 months ago.

CHAPTER 2 –

Comparing Notes

talked to my friend, Jackie, today. She's been divorced for almost two years now—wow, I can't believe it's been that long. Her only demise is that she still has to deal with her ex's traits that she hated when she was married. How she could live with a depressed alcoholic is beyond me! …and guess what? He's still at it. He's tried to kill himself at least twice since I've known her, and he still acts like he's going to do that crap when he doesn't get his way on any issue with his kids. My God, he's in his late 40s? What is he thinking? At least I don't have that to deal with that craziness. My only problem is that my soon-to-be-ex just couldn't keep it in his pants, and several people now know what he did.

The bad part is that my son doesn't know yet. He has several more days with his grandma in Texas. I'm sure he's having a great time there, but how will he react when he returns? I'm dreading next Tuesday when we have to tell him. A million scenarios have run through my mind on how to go through this, but none of them end well. I'm going to make my soon-to-ex tell our son that he has moved out. Don't get me wrong, I'll be there too, but I'm going to keep quiet for the most part. He started this; he can finish it! He can tell our son that he decided to leave because he has a new girlfriend since he cheated on his mother. I'm sure he won't say it to him in that respect, but it's really tempting for me to do it. However, I can't hurt our son the way his father hurt me. I just don't have it in me to be that way with anyone. I'm just taking each day at a time and trying to figure out what to do next.

Today, I had an inspiration—I bought a new book for my collection, *Divorce For Dummies*. It sounds a little strange, but I needed some guidance. The idea was originally a joke, but a friend told me that it did exist. At lunch time I headed to the bookstore, requested it by name, got a funny look from the clerk, and then purchased it and left. It seemed weird to buy this soft cover edition of something so valuable. Maybe I thought I'd never have to do this, but when a spouse cheats, your life is so upside down, everything is fair play.

At the end of the day, I took it home to contemplate my next move. I felt like I was playing a game of Chess—one wrong move and I was headed for disaster and I would lose. I was taking a gamble, but I read most of it and actually got some good advice. Was this my new sleeping pill? Could I now I get some sleep? There were way too many things to ponder now—bills, finances, taxes, division of assets, child support—the list went on. Concentrating on anything was impossible now—a flood of way too many things was now my enemy. My boss was even getting concerned and frustrated with me for my lack of attention. In addition to this mess, I need a knee operation. My world seems to be crumbling around me—but what about him? His world seemed to be locking into place one piece at a time. Of course, he had already rearranged his world with her prior to my knowing and made the pieces fit. But unlike him, my world came tumbling down.

The acid rain was all around me and I couldn't find shelter. I had enough stress in my life, and now I added more curricular activities to the pile—juggling this much stress wasn't my best trait. I mean, today after work, I went home and found some other dishes and some other things from the safe that were his possessions. I was nice enough to pack them up for him and await his return on Tuesday—you know the day when our son returns and we tear up his little world? Maybe I should have burned, boiled, or torched, or even thrown away his stuff, but somehow I kept my composure once again. I was going to be above his petty lies and deceit—if I had one thing, it was my pride. I hope I don't get to the point where I hate him with every inch of my life, but in the back of his mind, he may be thinking that thought. I guess the best thing about this mess is that I'm keeping a journal. I bought a 5-subject notebook and after less than 24 hours, I have 10 hand-written pages.

Day 6 – Today I'm still adding to my journal. In addition, I'm still losing weight and my knee is still hurting—so nothing's changed. Life still sucks! I wish I could get my surgery schedule figured out so that at least my physical pain could go away. There's just too much hurt in my life; both physical and mental that's causing me to lose control. But, as the days go by, my faith in God seems to grow stronger and with my friends, I know I will survive. Today, my thoughts go to "him" and how he is handling this mess he started. He's still out of town and far removed from this little town we're all a part of—at least physically. I guess being in another state might give him some air to breath—or perhaps not—I can only wish. They both still have to "face the music" soon. I'm not sure how they will handle it, because it has to be awkward. I guess, when you don't have any feelings in your entire body for anyone else in the world, it's easy. I even hoped his plane would crash—it might make my world a little better if God took him before his time. Was it mean to think those thoughts? Perhaps. I guess at the time, I didn't care and the word "hatred" was really in my vocabulary. Maybe I shouldn't have thought it, but wouldn't it be easier to tell our son that his dad died instead of telling him he cheated on his mother?

Day 7 – Today I feel a little better. My stomach is not in so many knots, but I'm still feeling somewhat overwhelmed. I did do a budget sheet to see if I can afford to live in my current home. The numbers came out ok; so I think I can make it by myself. I am also looking to see if I can get the house in my name only. I just wish "he" was in town so we could finish the paperwork before our son gets back from his trip. In addition, my thoughts still lean towards "her"—what is she currently thinking? Does she imagine that I will go ballistic and strike out at her in some way? Is she waiting for the day when we will meet in public, and she is preparing for something that may happen? I don't think she has any feelings of remorse, or anything else. I really don't. I wonder if someone "stole" her boyfriend in high school, or was it something that happened to her later in life that took away her respect for relationships? If the same thing happened to her why would she, on purpose, destroy so many lives? I guess the power of love, or in this case, lust, came first in both of their minds. The interesting part of this whole thing is that several of my co-workers know her. She has a business in town and is well known. Even though this town only consists of 25-35,000 people, it's still a small community. So, I'm sure the "word" will get around quickly. Plus, my co-workers were totally shocked at both of their actions. So, I don't understand why the both of them, who have so many community ties, would do something like this. She has a professional career that does business with my company. God, she's got nerve! They both do! Why would you put your reputation on the line for an affair? I almost, and I stress "almost," feel sorry for both of them. Maybe my compassion is unwarranted? At this point, anything goes.

In addition to my routine totally changing, I have decided to stop wearing my 3-stone diamond he gave me a few years back. He had replaced my wedding bands with that ring, and we had my wedding bands in the safe. Now, none of these rings mean anything. At first I wanted to keep them for my son. But now, the hurt is getting deeper and anything and everything annoys me about him—especially any ring he has ever given me. As for the rings, he stated that whatever I wanted to do with the bands was my decision, but he wanted to keep the antique diamonds from the wedding bands for our son. I agreed to do so. In addition to the ring dilemma, we put our son's name on the land we had purchased several years ago. They're just vacant lots, but its land we bought about two years after we were married. Now he's supposed to divide our investment accounts. There is so much to think of right now. All of the baggage a couple accumulates while they're married—it's totally amazing.

Can I stay calm until the 91st day hits? Because that's when it's supposed to be final, finito, done!! I just wish it were over now, today. How dare he put me in this position. Our vows meant nothing! I guess there was a reason I didn't put the word "obey" in those famous words we said to each other on that fateful day. It was supposed to be a 50/50 relationship; or at least I thought it was supposed to be that way. What was I thinking? Obviously, I was "WRONG" with a capital "W." I mean, we helped each other through my granddad's death and his grandmother's death while we were dating. We were even there for each other when both of our fathers passed away. We shared my happiness when I got out of the military, my college graduation, and the birth of our son. But, now that I look back, it was just after we sold our first home and I got pregnant that things began to change. Our other home was not finished yet, and since my ex was building most of the house, we lived with my mother-in-law to save money. Almost a year had passed before we were finally away from her and her rules, and we had our own home. This may have been the start of our demise. While we lived there, she constantly informed us that it was her house and her rules to live by. It became harder and harder to live with her as the days passed. At one point he, after working one job, and trying to build the new house, was at a point where he could stay down there. It was almost a 2-hour drive from his Mom's house, so now he had an excuse not to be in the same house and his mother, our son, and me. He stayed away as much as possible, or that's what it felt like.

Since he was a contractor, at the time, he was trying to do as much as possible without hiring someone to do the work on the new house. Needless to say, he was always tired and crabby due to the long days. Our fighting seemed to have started around that time, and being pregnant was the other addition to my attitude. I just remember going to work one morning when I was about seven months pregnant and wishing someone would hit my car so I would die, just to get away from him. I remember telling my mother in law, with tears in my eyes, about our fight just before I left for work. I was that unhappy.

In addition to my marriage troubles, this week Ed McMann, Farrah Faucet and Michael Jackson all died. Plus, my co-worker, Mary, also found out her husband was cheating, and another friend's husband was doing drugs. So, is this the week of tragedy or what? Do I want to cry or should I scream? After I heard of Michael Jackson's cardiac arrest and unfortunately death, my whole body was tingling. I mean, the other two were expected to die of their medical issues, but not a person so full of life and on a come back tour. What is happening to this world? It's almost a feeling that I had when 9/11 hit—shock, despair, and demise were all in my vocabulary. The last straw came when we had a very severe thunderstorm today—it's very gloomy in the world today—what's next?

All of a sudden I feel very alone. Every song I hear today, I find myself concentrating on every word. Each and every tune seems to have a different meaning than it did before. It's interesting and strange how life can change in an instant—I guess it's similar to a car accident. One second you're alive, and the next second everyone around you is dead. Life can change in an instant, but you're never prepared. The person you once were is changed forever—by the actions of others. May God help us all through this ever-changing world!

With everything happening in my life, I've also thought of going back to church instead of watching a church-televised program on TV. When I was with him, I felt as though I needed to change the channel on Sunday morning when he would walk into the room. Since he was so negative about religion, I didn't want to start another heated conversation. Why did I do the things I did to please him? He never did that for me. It seemed like it was he who came first all of the time, and I came second in every scenario. I never mattered to him, or did I just accommodate him too much? Too many questions to answer; why did I bother being with him this long?

These thoughts never seem to find their way out of my head-even when I'm at work. Plus when I finished today, I got a call from a girlfriend asking how I was doing. I told her that I was writing this journal to basically relieve my stress. We talked about several things, and then I got another call on my cell phone—it was my son. He told me of his day, but I don't know how much of it I heard for there were other issues I needed to deal with before he came home from Texas. I told him I really missed him and was looking forward to his return. He said he was ready to come home. This information just about broke my heart—if he only knew what was awaiting him upon his homecoming. My heart sank and I wanted to cry. I only spoke with him on my cell phone for a few minutes and then our conversation ended with me wondering my next move on how to tell him.

Turning on the local news was just as bad as dealing with this "divorce" thing. First there was the death of Michael Jackson and Farrah Fawcett, and now here was the Governor of South Carolina who was caught cheating on his wife. This was more bad news than I wanted to deal with today. Besides this news, they also talked about why men of power cheat on their wives. Does everyone know that I'm going through a divorce and everything around me should consist of bad news? It's all too much to think about sometimes, even though I think my ex must have been a politician in his former life; he acts just like one. In his job he has to deal with people, know a lot about how the world works, and know how to manipulate a situation to his advantage. He would be a perfect fit! This report also stated that testosterone was a powerful hormone that gives men a feeling of being invincible to the point where they think they will not be caught. My belief is that it's a feeling of wanting to be on a pedestal and always wanting to feel important and in charge. My belief is that failure is not an option for these men, so if it happens, they don't know how to cope. If life isn't going their way, they seem to grab a hold of something that makes them feel important and good about themselves, and sometimes it's not being with their spouse. So, why do men stray? Is the grass greener on the other side? They may think so at the time, but reality has to set in sometime in their lives.

Just after I wrote this last sentence, I thought I could put my pencil down. However, that was not the case. My mother called to check up on me and to inform me that my family never liked "him." Of course, she would say that, she's my mom! What mother would not take up for her child? She even told me that my brother even thought he was probably cheating for a long time. Was I blind? Did I ignore the warning signs and just go along with his quirks and ideas because he wanted things to be a certain way? I guess hind site is 20/20, for I can look back now and see that our relationship was not good for a very long time. For example, besides doing all of the indoor chores, near the end of our relationship, I started doing all of the outdoor chores as well. I guess I could give him some credit for trimming the trees twice in the last three years, but when we had first moved here, he did a lot to improve the property—a new fence, a new deck with a hot tub, planted several trees, and did a lot of landscaping in addition to a fish pond. When things weren't going his way, such as the pond leaking, and when the front fountain stopped working, he gave up and took them out. It was about that time, when his drive to keep up on the maintenance of his house died; along with our connection as husband and wife.

His drive may have originally started to dwindle when we first moved here, because he constantly said the phrase, "You made me sell my dream house." Well, he had mentioned selling his "dream house" well before we actually did, so this wasn't my fault—but perhaps I was his scope goat? He had to find someone to blame, and that someone was the person whose car was parked in the garage along with his truck—me! At that time, our house was in a wooded area off a dirt road.

The reason I wanted to sell was due to the fact that our son was about to start Kindergarten, and I wanted him to go to a school near were we lived. His elementary school was at least 10 miles away, and the bus stop was at least a half-mile away from our house. Since my job was 55 miles away, and I had to be at work at 7am, it was a little difficult for me to play "house mom." He, on the other hand, worked just 10 minutes away and basically refused to pull his weight to help out with our son. He said that he couldn't take our son to and from school, but that his job was first. Plus, he always said that I could get a closer job—I never could figure out where since the closest town had very few jobs that paid anything and had benefits. It seemed that for the first 12 years of my son's life, I did 99% of everything.

I remember one morning I was feeling like I was getting the flu and I had asked him to change our son's diaper. Well, of course, it had to be one of the "stinky" kind and all the way from the kitchen to his bedroom, I could hear "him" gagging and coughing because of the smell. He had a near death experience just by changing a diaper—I never heard the last of it! So after that, anytime when I was sick, had a migraine, or was otherwise predisposed, I just did everything for our son. Did I think he would ever help me with anything? Probably not at that point, because he didn't have any feelings of his own to relate to how I felt. He never offered to get up and help me at all. But, oh my, when he was sick, the whole world stopped spinning and someone had to take care of him.

Knowing what I know now, I should have left, but I don't know why I didn't. Maybe I didn't give up on a relationship; maybe deep down I knew I would never have what I needed....

<u>Day 8</u> – Today it still seems as if the world is realigning from the death of Michael Jackson. It was so sudden and not even I expected it. He must be on every television station and all over the

Internet. Farrah's death was expected and so was Ed McMann's, so my troubles seemed almost minuscule. I can't believe it's been seven days—one week—since I found out about his extracurricular activities. I've figured out now that it's not worth my time to confront his new chick. Why bother? What would it accomplish? However, an old saying comes to mind—"Give them enough rope and they will hang themselves." Maybe I can look into the future enough to realize that their relationship can't last due to how it started. How could a relationship start off on lies, deceit and messing around? What were they thinking with? It obviously wasn't with their heads atop their body. Did their physical and emotional ties in addition to their work ties help them make this decision? Maybe I'll never understand, or do I really want to know their reasons. Should I be bitter? Should I scream? I don't know how I should react. I think I'm numb. I have to put my emotions into something proactive—something that will improve my home life or improve my being.

At leave it's 4:30pm now, and the weekend is starting. I'll have a few days to myself after I drop off my son with his dad. I think I'm going to get a gallon of paint to paint the kitchen. It's something I've wanted to do for a long time now. I'm not doing this to make "him" mad, I just want to change my environment. If I have to live here for now, I want it to be "my place." My world was positioned around "him" so much and now his decision to change anything and everything in our lives leaves me at a loss. It was always about him—what he wanted to do and what I shouldn't do. Looking back, I wonder how I kept up appearances. Why did I allow myself to be so unhappy for all of those years? I guess I should have gotten out a long time ago, but perhaps I didn't know how to be on my own again. I guess financial reasons were to blame. For, where would I go? I definitely wouldn't go to his mother's house—the question was where? I never figured out an answer, so I was stuck. Perhaps, he did me a favor. The anchor he placed upon my back has now been removed, and now I'm not drowning in a sea of despair. I almost want to thank him. I'm glad I've had time to work through my emotions this past week. Perhaps, this will help me deal with his emotions better. Who knows, maybe I'll fall apart again or will I be stronger this time around? Time will only tell the truth of which is visible to the naked eye. I know I've been praying a lot more now than I had been in the past. I'm ready for some much-needed answers.

I'm beginning my decision- making process on my own. I even talked to a guy at a mortgage company to see what financing opportunities I might have. I want to get on with my life—but what will my future hold? My story is just beginning when it comes to the rest of my life. I even, just for revenge; want to date a cop just because he hates cops and what they stand for. I guess he is sort of a rebel and likes to flaunt the law to the limit. As for me,

I'm still getting my mindset—at least now I'm not worried if he's cheating or not, for the truth has reveled itself. I know now that my suspicions were all true. Part of me wants payback and the other half knows his new relationship will fail and fail miserably. Oh well, it wasn't me that cheated! It now brings new meaning to thinking the grass is greener on the other side. I just wonder what her daughters think. They're just teenagers (one in high school and the other in college), and I know he thinks they're just "divas." I know this because he expressed those feelings from being at her house when he finished her basement, and he came home one night to say he was glad we had a son, because he couldn't stand being around teenage girls. I give their relationship until Christmas before all hell breaks loose. He'd better not try to crawl back to me—I'm done with his crap, and I'm moving forward without him.

CHAPTER 3 –

The New Routine

I t's now 3:30 p.m. and I'm still at work. I can't wait until 4:30 gets here until I can leave. I'm getting anxious again. It helps to have this journal with me at all times so I can vent when I feel the urge. With all the sleep I've lost in the last week and it being the weekend again, I have several emotions looming within me. I feel afraid to be alone, but at the same time, I enjoy it. I miss my son, but when he comes home from his trip, how will he react? How dare his father do this to us? However, it's refreshing for me to be by myself, because now I don't have to deal with his attitude anymore and fear what he will say again each and every time he comes home or each time he leaves. I had a boss one time who gave me enough ups and downs; I don't need any more

37

attitude from anyone; especially now. The scary thing is that a former boss was just like him. I used to get "it' from work and then get "it" at home—no wonder I was miserable, and this happened years ago before this mess. This is hard enough and I can't turn it on then off—"it" being my feelings. I have a hard time doing that. If I'm upset, it succumbs my whole being. It's hard to think of anything else. I have feelings and compassion for people—this former boss could be cold; just like him. They both can turn on and off their emotions like a water facet. I brewed steam over the slightest problem for a long time. Maybe I'm too sensitive; maybe I'm just gullible? It's just the way I am, and I have to deal with it.

<u>Day 9</u> – its Saturday. One week ago I busted him and he admitted to an affair with her. However, I can't think of that nightmare right now. For today, I am continuing to paint the kitchen and the family room. I hate the red color in the family room. It reminds me of him and how he used to yell at me, so I have to get rid of that reminder. Now, I'm on a mission to continue painting from last night and get it done. It's now after 9 a.m. and I hear a strange noise that sounds like something in the garage. My curiosity got the best of me, so I had to go and check. After opening the door leading to the garage, I found that the garage door was open. I know I closed it last night. I had checked it twice and even locked the door coming into the house from the garage. Now I'm a little spooked and concerned for my safety. Am I being paranoid?

I don't think so, and on that thought, I decided to look through the house file and find the information on the garage door code instructions. After getting the paperwork, I proceeded downstairs to get the ladder. The instructions were a little confusing at first, but after a while, I figured them out. I changed the access code to the door and to the garage door opener. I was so proud of myself! I could do what he could do, and I didn't need him to do it. As I finished, I noticed my next-door neighbor talking to a neighbor down the street. I walked down to their truck and informed them what had happened. They gave their condolences and listened as I vented. I realized later that I was just like one of those "wives" that bitched and moaned about their ex. I guess they were curious why he was never around, but now they knew. The cat was out of the bag. Did they have any idea what a jerk he was to me? Probably not, but I needed to just let it go. Besides, I was out of paint by now, and I had to go get more.

Of course my situation must have some humor, right? So, on that note, I realized that God has a sense of humor because the paint that I just bought was the wrong tint. So, after realizing this I went back to the store to return it. The guy tried two more times to re-create it, and then he realized the computer program he used to re-create it kept messing up the color I needed. Maybe God is trying to get my mind off my heartache. But when I returned the second time, I started thinking of my son. He gets home in three days. This just made my stomach turn. There again was that gut-renching feeling I had had all week. How am I going to tell him? What will his reaction be? He's such a caring little boy and tears come easily to him. For example, when we had to put down his dog over a year ago, he asked where he was after his dad took him to his place of death. I had to tell him he was gone; his dad had to put him down. There were instant tears and it just broke both our hearts. However, this is bigger and more intense with bigger changes than he's ever dealt with before. I just pray for more strength than I've ever had in my life.

It's evening and I grilled some chicken for dinner. I really haven't felt like eating lately, and as of today, I've lost four pounds since I last got on the scale. At the rate I'm going, I'm going to look really good when "D" day hits. As for her, she could lose a few pounds too. It was interesting to fix dinner, and then turn around to the family room to see the red color is now gone— now it's covered by a sandy brown tone. The loudness of the room has been subdued. I even had those same thoughts again that his plane could crash (since he's coming home today). Am I wrong to think so badly? Maybe I want revenge so much that I wish I could hurt my "soon to be ex" as much as he hurt me. Is that wrong? Do I really hate him for what he did to me? There are so many emotions rolling around in my head right now, that I can't even think straight. One part of me feels sorry for him because I know in my heart his new love interest won't weather the storm. I know she won't. I mean, how do you start off a relationship like this? Besides, her "diva" daughters will eventually get on his nerves. So, now he wants to be a "step dad"? Hell, he can't even be a real husband and father—what makes him think he can take on a new role— especially to step daughters? I think both of them are nuts! Nevertheless, everyone's lives have changed due to their actions.

As for me, my inner peace and quiet I feel right now will not last. Next week will be filled with a lot of grief; I am going to be sad, depressed, torn—I just know it. I don't want to anticipate my sadness, but it's coming. It's like knowing a death is about to occur. How does anyone ever deal with that thought? No one ever prepares you for that moment in your life where everything changes. If we all knew when bad things were going to happen, we would all be walking around like zombies or on eggshells. This has got to be the most difficult thing I've ever done. Am I a failure in some way? Maybe. But, at least I can hold my head up high and say I didn't cheat on my spouse.

If he was so miserable, why didn't he say something sooner? My theory is that they became "buddies," enjoyed hanging out with each other, and then with one quick lightening bolt, realized their relationship was more than just friends. But, what bothers me most is that he kept denying the responses from people around

41

him that they were "together." For example, I remember once when my son and I went to his office on a Friday evening looking for him to see if he wanted to go to dinner, but he was not there. His co-worker told me that he was at a local pub. Well, we left his office and headed down the street to that location. My first thought was that he was with a client—since he frequented this place many times with his clients. But, low and behold, as I opened the door, there he was at the bar with her just sitting casually. He said they were just talking business. Since my son and I were getting pizza down the street, I invited them, but they declined. They both didn't want to leave—I should have realized then, that they were an item. Why didn't I see it then? Men can have women as friends, right? I guess not in my case when one is married and the other is not. Also, he once told me that someone asked them if they were married when they were together at the bar, and his response was, "I'm married, but she's not." This came out of his mouth like he was astonished someone would say it about the two of them.

Was she after him from the beginning? I guess when those two had initially met, she had a boyfriend, but she later broke up with him. This same situation happened to me when I was in my 20s. My roommate and I both had boyfriends when we first became roommates. She later broke up with her boyfriend, and started seeing my boyfriend since my relationship was going nowhere. She did it behind my back when I was out of town for two weeks, and then she ended up marrying him. Why did she move in on my turf? To this day I don't know the answer, but all I do know is that it was wrong. I was just glad that I was getting transferred to Washington, D.C, and I was out of the situation. The only bad part was that I had a couple of weeks before I left and the tension between my roommate and me was like cutting through a brick. I felt so betrayed by both of them. Maybe that's why I never did anything like that to anyone else I've ever known. It definitely cut like a dagger, and it was very cruel to me. I have more scruples than that! I wasn't raised to hurt someone that badly, ever! I just wonder where the morals in the world are now? Has the 21st century turned us against each other?

Day 10 – It's Sunday and there's only two more days until my son returns home. I so want to tell him that his dad is a cheat and a liar, but as I think those thoughts, a "calming" feeling comes over me. Maybe it's the fact that I've kept busy today. I finished my painting and cleaned behind the refrigerator, swept and mopped the floor, in addition to mowing the lawn, doing two loads of laundry, and cleaning up the back yard. I think I'm too tired to be mad or upset. However, I still need to iron my clothes for work this week. Just think, I used to do all this for "him," and I never got a "thank you" or a "great job" comment out of his mouth. He, on the other hand, used to brag about the work he did outdoors and in his job. I used to pick up his clothes from the floor, wash and iron them, and in addition to this, I would get comments like, "Where are my glasses," or "Where are my shoes?" Or, another one was, "That's just looks bad!" I was never good enough for him. All I was to him was a maid. He always wanted more from me than he ever gave, and each and every time my efforts were not up to his standards.

I guess a leopard never loses his spots—his new chick will find that out soon enough. She has a career, so I see her getting sick of his sloppy ways real quick. But, I've also thought that perhaps she won't. She's obviously in love with him—enough to put up with his irritating ways that used to drive me crazy. Love must be blind. So, I'm guessing six months from now he'll be finding a new place to live? By that time, I want to publish this journal and have revenge or satisfaction—either one will work!

This weekend was far too long. Maybe its because I've accomplished so much. This house is becoming my house—not "our house," but mine. I even bought a new clock today only because the other one broke. I'm sure he would have had a comment about that too. The old one was white, cheap and ugly. I now have a gold rustic one with a black center that looks good against my new sandy-colored walls. I have so many plans for this place. I want to replace the ceiling fan in the living room, in addition to the carpet on the first level. I also want to change the lights in the dining and living room, the outside lights, get rid of the broken hot tub and extend the deck where it once was and put up a porch swing. I almost feel as if my life is blooming once again. I'm sure he'll have some comments when he comes over on Tuesday—he always does. I'll let him know that we each need to deal with life in our own way, and now is my way! I'm sure he'll have one last "jab" in before he's through with me. He complained that his mother always did that to him, and I think unconsciously, he's always done that to me without realizing it. However, I think it's just an excuse—he's never had to deal with his childhood the way he should have, and I don't think he'll ever be happy. Even when we got engaged years ago, all of his friends couldn't believe the "President of the He Man Woman Haters Society," had finally been caught. Then, years afterwards, his friends didn't believe we could still be married because of the way he acted to people in general. I constantly got asked how I could stand him. I would always reply, "I just ignore him." There was one thing that I couldn't ignore; he never had the common courtesy to let me know where he was if he was out late. He would always tell me that it was like he was checking in with his mother, so he usually didn't call to tell me when he would be home. I guess the old saying is true, that a man will treat his wife like he treats his mother. I can't believe how blind I was for so many years! Was I that naïve? Or, was I just too young and stupid to care?

It's Monday—just one week and two days since it happened. Tomorrow my son comes home. Yes, he comes home and to what? To a mom and dad who are going to break the news that his life will change forever from the one he's always known! So, it's one more night of freedom for me, at least one more night I'm alone in this house. It feels weird—no one to account to; no one to ask permission—for everything that I do. I'm sure I'll get comments about this new look in the house. My son is his dad's image—he can't stand change either. I'm sure his first reaction will be one of, "What were you thinking?" But, that won't last long—I am woman hear me roar? Right? How will he react? Will I first see tears streaming down his face? Will there be confusion? He's only 13 years old—on one hand he's still my baby, but on the other, he's going through puberty. This is the last thing he needs in addition to being a teenager.

I have to stay strong—I guess we all do. Even though I want to rip my ex's eyes out, he is my son's father. He did give me a loving and kind young man who would do anything for anyone. My son's been there for my every whim when I had my surgery for my neck, and for my knee operation. Too many thoughts were going through my mind, so after work, I just had to call him and let him know I loved him and really missed him. Little did he know his world would soon fall apart?

As I looked back at today, while at work, I felt pretty good. I was more focused than I have been. I even felt like I had a new goal in life. I feel so empowered today—there are so many things I want to accomplish now. I know that the spell has been lifted but the floodgates will open tomorrow. Sometimes I catch myself with the reality that my life has changed forever. It's kind of scary, but it's also exciting. Now, I'm going to be responsible for all the bills to include the house, insurance, utilities, and whatever else I accumulate. God help me!

It's Tuesday—the day my son gets back. I'm still torn on how to handle this situation, because, last night I talked to my mother-in-law and I really got confused. I think she's really torn between her son and me. Her loyalty is split between the two of us. She seemed, at first, to be neutral about the whole situation, but now I don't know. I did tell her that it was her son who wanted to move out and be with "her." I think she was surprised when I told her of that information. I mean, as a mom you want to believe that your child is perfect—well not in this case. I guess both of us need to sit down, far away from my son, and talk. I hope she'll be open to all that has happened. Whom will she believe? I guess that's the million-dollar question right now. Even though she and her son don't see eye to eye a lot of the time about many things and they often fight, I tried to stay out of it. However, I always got drug into the middle of their arguments. Will she yell at him? Will she blame him or even me? Only time will tell, but tonight will be the end and even the beginning of my worry.

As I drove to work this morning, I kept thinking about this mess. I almost want to thank him for giving me my freedom back. I haven't even had a migraine headache from this whole mess; which surprises me. That's rare for me to get this stressed and not deal with a massive headache. What has this done for me? Have I finally realized my full potential since I was so stifled? This feeling is hard to talk about. For, freedom is a scary thing. It's not like it was when I was a teenager or when I graduated from high school, but I'm now in my 40s. Something's changed, and speaking of high school, my 30th class reunion is this August. I didn't plan to go, but I was going to write a letter to my classmates. But, now, what will I say? Do I have to tell them anything? No, I don't! Even though I've changed the voice mail on my home number, the garage door combination, taken his name off some of the bills, I still feel beholding to him. There's just too much to think about, but each minute tells a new tale.

Well, I got to work, and guess what? I got word that he now wants to wait until tomorrow to tell our son. He doesn't want to ruin his vacation by hitting him in the face with the "news." Is he being a coward? He wants to wait until tomorrow after he takes him to a doctor's appointment so we can all be together. I hesitated doing this, but he does have a small point—let him settle back into his routine first. I don't like the idea of "covering" for him until tomorrow. I mean—a lot of his belongings are gone already. So, I guess I'm supposed to lie about where everything went! Now, I'm the bad guy. Well, if he wants 50/50 custody, he's going to get it. I also let him know that our son has three appointments this month and two of them fall on "his" weeks. I can just see it now that he will put this off onto me, or "her" in some form or fashion. I can just imagine that she will get tired of this quickly. That's ok—just give me back my son. There are several bad words that I have in my vocabulary at this moment, and most of them four letters long—Jerk!

More emotions are going through my mind today at work— several scenarios that I thought could happen. But, I was surprised before lunch; he has agreed to take our son to his hearing appointment and another appointment next Monday. He wants me to take our son to his eye exam and to his dentist, or he would get his mom to do it. What's with him? Did he get time to himself since last Wednesday to think what he wants out of life? Did he clear his head to the point that he knows where he's going now? I think not. He's at a preliminary point in his life with his new "chickypoo"—and as he said, he's basically at a point in his life where he was 20 years ago—he's starting over. Well, join the club, dude! All I can say is "Whaaaa!" Maybe that's how I'm dealing with this whole thing—writing it down and venting to my friends. Just getting it out to someone who is on my side is helping tremendously. I just don't want to inundate them with so much information that they don't want to be around me. My circle of girlfriends has been my saving grace. If I didn't have them, I'm not sure what I'd do. Even though I feel I've always been a strong person overall, there are times now that I can't deal with life's little issues. Perhaps, it's my stubbornness that makes me prevail.

Well, my day at work has ended. He went to pick up his mom and our son from the airport. Of course, he was a chicken and said nothing, and then dropped them off at his mom's house. She just lives down the block, so she's close, and just as I left work, I got the call from my son to pick him up there. As I arrived at her house, my heart sank as I saw him. I wanted to tell him so much, but I made up an excuse for him to go get his grandma's mail. Just seconds after he left, I proceeded to tell my mother-in-law how I caught her son and how I suspected him of cheating. She told me that I was pretty good at hiding my feelings since I never spoke about what I assumed. I informed her that I was pretty sure this was going on for quite a while. I also reassured her that I wanted her in our son's life since she was such an important person to him. Her reaction was good, but I'm not sure if she wondered if I hated her too just because she was related to him. She must have been in shock—who wouldn't be? Well, we left after my son came back from the mailbox and on the way home, my son immediately told me that his dad had class tonight and wouldn't be home. As we pulled into the garage, he noticed that the tool cabinet and some tools on the workbench were also gone. He was getting a little concerned, but I told him that his dad moved some things around—there I go, lying again! He even noticed in the kitchen that the coffee pot was missing. I told him it was broken. Why was I lying, again? I felt like such a hypocrite. Damn him for putting me into this situation! He's living a lie and now I'm a part of it! How dare he put me through more crap just because he wants things a certain way. I hate him for doing this to me again. What's going to happen when my son sees his dad's dresser gone too? I had to go outside and chill. I ended up watering the grass while I called a girlfriend. She was disgusted that he would chicken out tonight—of all nights! Just wait until tomorrow. If he doesn't tell him—I will. But if he does, I'm going to let him do most of the talking. I can't believe I have to go through this one more day.

It's Wednesday—I sent him an e-mail this morning asking him if he could pay me the child support he promised when he comes over this evening. I never heard anything, and before I knew it, half the day was gone. I eventually called him, and he actually answered his phone—amazing! I can get in touch with him more now than when we lived under the same roof. He said he'd come over around 5:15, and then we'd tell our son the "news." So, after work I picked up my son from his grandmother's house and then proceeded home. Our son informed me that he thought that dad would be home around 9 p.m. or so. Well, I told him that it would probably be sooner than that. I pulled into the garage and was quickly becoming anxious. I walked outside onto the deck and within five minutes I saw his truck turn the corner. I immediately walked to the front door, but I was too late. He had come in through the door leading to the garage. I walked back inside and heard a knock. Well, there he was—my first reaction was to run away and quickly. I didn't want to be in the same room as this man, for I knew what was coming. But, I was pleasantly surprised when his first reaction was that he liked the new paint on the walls. It must have been just minutes and then our son heard his dad so he came downstairs. He came into the kitchen with us, and then the bomb dropped. His dad started off by reminding our son that he and I have been fighting a lot lately, and that now we've decided to live in separate houses. Our son asked twice where his dad would be living, and he told him that he would be at "her" house, and "Yes," our son knows "her." They had both been over to "her" house on several occasions. Now the confusion began—the tears were welling up in my son's eyes and he became agitated. He walked around in a state of confusion and then grabbed a store ad that was nearby. He was acting like he wanted to read it to make this news go away. He was visibly upset, but we both gave him hugs and told him this was the best for everyone. His dad then told him he wanted to take him out for dinner to talk. I thought they were going out to dinner by themselves, well, I found out later that they both went over to "her" house for dinner. Who does something like that? My God, he just introduced our son to his mistress!! This woman is no longer his friend, but his girlfriend. Doesn't he have any shame? He should have had one-on-one time with our son, not tell him that she is his new "stepmother." The other thing that was too traumatic was that they had picked out paint for our son's room, since he didn't like the paint that I had painted in his room recently. He broke the news that this new paint was for his room over there. OMG! What a blow to anyone's psyche!

I felt so sorry for my son now—and when he brought our son home, he got the rest of the boxes from the garage as our son watched. The boxes were slowly put into his truck and after just a few minutes he was gone. What did he tell our son? I mean, what did she say to him that evening? Are they both proud of their actions? What type of parental role models are they displaying? I was so angered and distraught from this, that I just didn't know what to do, and after his dad left, my son went to his room to gather some items to take over to his new room at her house. I know the confusion was setting in—with whom would he now have his loyalty? He was handed a blow that no teenager wants to ever deal with. He was so distraught; he ended up laying these items on his bed and kept them there all night as he slept.

CHAPTER 4 —

My Son The Victim

oday is Thursday, July 3, 2009. These last two weeks have been exhausting. My sleep patterns are all messed up. Plus, for the last two days we've been short-handed at work. So, I'm helping in another department more than usual, and today we had a meeting that I had to help set up, so it's been quite busy. In addition, my thought patterns are confused. I just couldn't wait for the day to end—I'm tired. As I left work, then arrived home, I awaited the arrival of my son. His grandma is going to drop him off this evening. When he came through the door, I was cleaning out the guinea pig cage. After putting the wood chips into their home, we began speaking about these new changes. He was very open about his feelings. Maybe it helped by me leaving him a note this morning that we both loved him very much and that this was not his fault. I also told him that he could talk to me about anything. I've always tried to be honest with him or at least very close to the truth so he wouldn't get hurt. It's hard to be a kid and every age has its challenges. Besides, divorce isn't easy for adults, let alone kids. Then, if something else like drugs and alcohol are involved—it's even worse.

I guess my situation is better than most. For example, one of my girlfriends who has been divorced for almost two years has an ex that tried to kill himself twice and he also abuses alcohol. The letter "L" is definitely stamped upon his forehead, but I don't think he knows that. My other friend's husband was doing drugs, and now she's also filed for divorce. It seems that lately men are losing their minds. Do women have to keep their sanity for their kid's sake? Is it that the recession is causing men to run out on their wives? I see it at work all the time. I've even seen women running out on their husbands. The client's we serve at work have needs well beyond what affects me. So, I do feel somewhat fortunate that my soon-to-be ex and I get long somewhat better now than we have in a long time. However, one thing my son said tonight surprised me—he said his dad told him that he was never getting married again. For some reason, I don't believe that. If he can lie and cheat with another woman who was once his friend, she'll convince him otherwise. I'm sure she had a lot to do with the "cheating" part of their relationship.

Two weeks ago, I didn't think I'd be in this "calm" period of my life. I feel an inner peace that didn't exist before. I don't know why. The only thing that still bothers me is my financial situation. I want to get the house out of his name, but that's still in the works. Most of the bills are currently being transferred into my name so the process has at least begun. The investments are what I want to know about and how much money we have to split. As for the house, he said that he would look over the contract to see if it was fair. Go figure? Now, he's being nice to me! Then, once that is done, next is the parenting class that we both have to attend—seems like a good waste of $60 if you ask me. After everything is submitted to the court, then comes the waiting period for "D" day. It seems like such a long time to get rid of that anchor you despise so much. Will I feel really free and besides, what does "free" mean for me? Who knows? My emotional roller coaster is so over the map, but, I want to have that control over my life as I did before I met him and said, "I do." So, I may even get a cat tomorrow from the animal shelter.

Plus, I remember giving up my feline when I married him because he was allergic. What was I thinking? I gave up a part of myself to fit into his world. The next man I let into my life will honor me and will accept my pets as well as my child. My compromises will be few, and this time I won't lose myself in the process. It's got to be 50/50 or nothing. I want someone to treat me as good or better than his parents and/or siblings. I think I deserve at least that much. I am not playing maid to anyone again!

It's now Friday and today we split the cost of a bed for our son for his new place. Of course, he didn't want to shop for the best deal—for once in his life, so it will be a little costly. He's expecting me to go 50/50 on everything, even clothes. I know my son needs clothes--even over there. So "he" decided to make our son more comfortable by having the same things at each residence. Now I'm paying twice for everything that I once was— it was me who bought everything for our son. I even paid for all of the medical and dental expenses, for the first 13 years of his life. This doesn't include all of the daycare expenses that I paid for when others cared for him. OMG! He has finally stepped up to the plate and he's finally getting off his butt? Did he feel guilty about his actions and is now trying to redeem himself through our son? I mean he was planning on leaving me! But, guess what? I busted him first! In addition, I guess, according to him we're going to go over finances sometime this week. He just has to still be in control somehow! It must be a guy thing. That conversation will be tense—I can see it now. Besides, there's more paperwork to do and we have to file it soon and who knows what that will cost.

Today is Saturday. I have planned an outing with my son today to the Renaissance Festival. We had some time to talk on the way there, but before we left I let him know that his dad and his "chick" may hug or kiss because their new relationship may warrant that emotion. His immediate response was, "Well I'll just ask dad to take me home." When he said that, my heart just sank. I just wanted him to know the situation he's getting into over there. I'm not lying to him anymore. I'm sure I'll hear from "him" that I'm putting our son up to something. Just wait—it's coming. I was hoping that today would be uneventful, but as we were participating in the Fair's activities, one of the male vendors called me, "My Love." My son immediately responded, "No, she's not your love, she's mine!" Wow! I guess he's the only male in my life right now that is coming to my rescue. He's even giving me more hugs lately—this has got to be hard for him. We talked also, about how different it will be over there. I hoped that our conversations would be calming for him but as for me, I kept noticing all the families. There were young families with young children; and seniors who probably have been together for years. There weren't any women with just their kids. Was I the only one whose husband was on a "cheating spree?" It was a very lonely feeling. I even watched one young family who were playing with their kids and taking pictures of each other. I want that back again, but not with him. We hadn't been really "together" for quite a while. He hasn't wanted to kiss or even hug me for so long that I wasn't sure when we had been that close. We hadn't been "together' in the bedroom for at least two years. It may have started when I was in a car accident about five years ago and hurt my back. Having an intimate relationship from then on was painful. Although the spark lowered, I thought we still had a marriage. Little did I know what he was really doing? In reality, I don't think he started this affair—I think he really thought of her as just a friend—so this tells me she was just as guilty as he.

It's Sunday—the day my son goes over to her house. How can he take my baby, my flesh and blood from me for one whole week? I know my son doesn't want to go—it will be really hard for him. I mean he can't even find a new pair of shoes for his son at the department store! How can he take care of a child? As for the shoes, he just gave up to easily, got bored, and left the store. After one store didn't have his size, so he just gave up and said that he would get them later. Well, if he wants 50/50 custody, he's going to get an eye full. I know he hasn't realized how much I take care of our son. Do men ever realize how much their wives take care of their children? Well, obviously, not in my case. Granted, there are men out there that do put forth the effort, but my ex wasn't one of them. He was so much into himself and the "I" word came up so often, it made me sick. Maybe it's my military background—the word "I" didn't exist. We had to be a team in order to survive. I just can't believe I thought this man was my soul mate—and get this—we met through a dating service! It was the joke for a long time that "those things never work!" I guess they don't if one of the two people is a sociopath. Don't get me wrong; he wasn't always like that. At one point, I was a very important part of his life; it's just been the last 10+ years that he or "we" changed. It seemed as if I had to ask permission for everything I wanted to do. He "told" me what he was going to do, so there was no "50/50" there at all. Additionally, he constantly told me that whatever I wanted to do, such as go back school, for a particular profession, I wouldn't be successful and make a lot of money. I guess he was right with everything in my life—NOT!

Life got to the point that anything I wanted to do was wrong and his way was correct. Was it the fact that his dad always stifled him in his aspirations? According to him, it was. Why then did the lies start between us? Well, a few years back he bought a motorcycle and then proceeded to tell me, for the next six months, that it was his friend's bike who was hiding his assets from his soon-to-be ex wife. Why did he start this? He even got mad at me when I bought a new vehicle and didn't ask permission from him. Then, he proceeded to rip up my sales paperwork and yell at me. Perhaps my motive was to get back at him for lying to me. Maybe I was tired of the "obey" part of the wedding vows of which I didn't repeat at the ceremony. That word was very offensive to me, and now I know why. That word shouldn't be in a relationship if it is a 50/50 commitment—it wasn't that way from the start from when we first dated. So, then why did I put up with that crap for too many years? Was it the fact that I was young and stupid? I was 29 years old when I married him—I wasn't just naïve and straight out of Catholic School. I thought I was pretty knowledgeable about life; I guess I wasn't. The other thing he did was to take out a $27k second from the house and pay what he called "cash" for his new truck—all without my permission. Then he proceeded to brag that he paid cash for his vehicle, and I would have to keep my car for at least five more years; I couldn't buy anything until then. Was this man arrogant or what?

There never seemed to be anything in our relationship to where we had any compassion for each other; he didn't respect me and I was definitely down the path to not respecting him anymore. It also just seemed as if he made up his own rules for the past few years. Was he grabbing at straws to make himself feel better? I guess some men do that; I don't know. I really believe he needs counseling in order to deal with his past demons from his childhood. He's on a self-destructive course and the only thing that's keeping him on track is our son. I just don't want our son to be his dad's pawn in order to save his life and put him back on the right course. I also believe that if he got his values and morals in check, he could feel better about himself and really flourish. Also, if his ego could calm down, he really would be pleasant to be around. In addition, he has always looked at his friends' successes and bragged about them. I once confronted him and asked if he was jealous. He denied it, but I knew better. I guess it's just in a guy's demeanor to want to succeed so that people look up to you—well, who wouldn't want that? It's just that when someone your same age is more successful than you, and that person just happens to be a close friend, it does make you feel a little insecure and perhaps a little jealous. Perhaps some of his actions were based on his early education that confused him. But with him, his Baptist school education "force fed" him too much of the bible—at least that's what he said. This part of his life really seemed to have affected him a lot. He is really resentful when it comes to anyone mentioning God. As the years went by in our marriage, he got more and more angry and started to deny God's existence. Was it that he thought his background, education and missed opportunities cause his demise and he hadn't arrived at the ultimate financial and emotional security point in his life? Was it everyone else's fault that he didn't become a millionaire before he was 30 years of age? I really believe that fantasy and reality have become intertwined with him. He has high hopes and that's great to hold within you and have as goals. However, it seemed like he didn't get it somehow. When I knew things weren't going to happen, as he wanted, was this a disappointment to him? Or was it another one of life's tests that he failed, once again? Don't get me wrong, I wish him well, and I also have my faults—

I'm not perfect either. However, I think I handle disappointment better than he did, for I was mostly a realist. I didn't fanaticize that things were going to be a certain way when I knew for certain that they could never be his way. I guess my strong will to survive has served me well.

Today was hard; he came to get our son this morning before lunch. My son called him just after breakfast because he didn't know what time the "pick up" was scheduled. Within 15 minutes there he was in his pickup truck that was breaking down. This moment went ok—I actually got a thank you for helping with the cost of the bed we bought for his house. But, today was different; all of the "thank you" compliments just went out the window for me. I didn't care about anything else—my son was leaving me again for a week. It seemed like yesterday he was gone to Texas for 10 days. All his life he hadn't been far from my side. The tears in my eyes said it all; I just hope my son does ok there. I even told my soon-to-be ex that our son had a lot of questions and for him to be honest with him.

After a quick hug from my son, he was gone. I saw him drive away and my heart sank into the pavement. I know I had to do something with my time, and feeling sorry for myself was inexcusable. My first thought was that I should go for a drive, so I eventually ended up at the hardware store. I had my second project planned. With a sander, cordless drill, paint and supplies,

I was ready to tackle the kitchen cabinets. This painting project was to compliment the painting project of last week. I had always hated the look of those cabinets. You know, the "old" dirty oak look—Yuk! Now, I don't have any excuse to not make them shine. After sanding down and painting two doors, my neighbor called to see how I was doing. She invited me for a late lunch, I guess, to check up on my mental progress. She's always been a great ally to me. We've shared some great conversations in the past and especially within the last two weeks because of my impending divorce. Nonetheless, she even told me that she supports whatever decisions I make due to financial issues or whatever else might come up. Everyone should have a friend like her! I hope that I never get to the point where I need him to live with me, ever again, for financial reasons or for my son's sake. It would never work. Cheating and lying are at the top of my list for not being married in addition, to anyone ever raising their hand to me. I cannot abide by any man hurting me in that respect; no woman should have to put up with that nonsense.

She even let me know that her marriage is on the rocks. They're just co-existing or co-habiting in the same house. I know her pain—Hell, I'm there now! I guess going through the emotions is just the next step to divorce. It's like a disease around me lately. We're all in the same boat in my neighborhood; there's too much of this "break up" thing going on around here.

CHAPTER 5 —

The New Norm

wo days have past and I'm keeping busy by sanding and painting the kitchen cabinets every night after work until almost 8pm. Another bright spot was that my son sounded better today when I called him. He and his Grandma went shopping and they had a good time. I get to see him tomorrow; it's our mid-week dinner together. I'm going to pick him up and bring him home to my place to eat dinner. It will be a short night, but I miss him dearly—this outing will help break up the week. I'm sure he'll say something to his dad about my extra curricular activities in the kitchen. My first thought was, if his dad was still there and I had done this project, there would have been Hell to pay. My second thought was "who cares. I'm doing something I've always wanted to do, but didn't because of him. I'm now "free," right? To a certain extent, yes, but why does my stomach feel so unsettled? I mean I have to take my son back to her house tomorrow after dinner. What kind of woman fools around with a married man? Does she think she can hold onto him forever? I have more scruples in my right pinkie than she does in her whole body. Am I jealous? Not really. I just want someone in my life, eventually, to love me like I feel everyone should have the right to be loved. I want to love them back the same way! I know it will happen someday. I hope that day is soon.

It's Wednesday; the day I get to see my son. He called me earlier in the day, and I think he is excited that I'm coming to get him. I picked him up at his Grandma's who had gotten Chinese food for us. We left her house to my place, and after we arrived he immediately went to see his guinea pigs. I know he missed his pets, for he usually wasn't far from them for very long. But now, it's different, he doesn't have any pets over there, so I know he needs a neutral zone to escape to and that's why he wants to be with them. After visiting for a while, he immediately proceeded to eat dinner in his room. He always liked to do that, but tonight it seemed he wanted to escape to his retreat. I went upstairs to talk to him and as he saw me, he turned off his TV in his room. I tried to get him to open up, but I think he's torn between the loyalties he has for both of us. He even had a hard time talking as we left his Grandma's house. It's as if he's betraying our trust if he even spoke about either one of us. I did get him to talk, because every time I'm with him in a one-on-one conversation, I stress to him that I love him and that he could tell me anything. I want him to feel comfortable telling me what he feels—good or bad. He did open up for a brief moment to tell me that he had trouble sleeping over there at his dad's new place. After that brief encounter, he clammed up once again. He even wanted to leave early and have Grandma take him over to his dad's place instead of me. Was he trying to protect me from her? Does he think there might be a scene if we encounter each other? Maybe he knows something I don't. I don't know how I will react to her when we finally do meet face to face. Will I freeze, or will my tongue say something I will regret? I know this woman for God's sake! Someone I thought was just an associate of his. How does she sleep at night? If I had done something like this, I would be filled with so much shame, I wouldn't be able to live with myself! Was it the way I was raised? Of course it was—sometimes my anger gets so great, I'm ready to hit something because of their actions. Other times, I just vent to my friends and the anger will fizzle away. When I'm by myself, I think I'd go crazy if I didn't have a project to complete. Thank goodness I'm refinishing the cabinets at this point in time.

Today is the fourth straight day I've worked on the cabinets, and tonight I stopped my project early. By 8pm, I just couldn't do it anymore. I'm tired, and sleep is what I crave. If those dang birds outside my window would stop singing at 4:30 a.m. every morning, I'd be ok. I'm not in the mood to be happy today. My life has been turned upside down and my emotions are still raw. It's just too hard to describe, but what I'm feeling is so real. I feel like I need guidance, but I don't know where to turn right now; maybe, soon I'll figure it out.

Today is Thursday, and I feel pretty good. My spirits were high, at least until I had been at work for about 30 minutes. A co-worker of mine, Mary, had caught her husband calling and texting another woman—13 calls between the two of them, with one of the calls happening on her birthday! I had noticed that she seemed different in the past few days. Even her facial features appeared different; perhaps she wasn't wearing any mascara? Or was she crying? I didn't say anything to her—maybe I should have. She looks devastated. I knew her life was changing rapidly in the past few months. Her ex had lost his job, and then they moved into an apartment from renting a house to save money. Now this! She said she knows the other woman—just like me. She also said that her and her husband really haven't talked much lately, but should have. He kept telling her that they needed to sit down and discuss something, but they never took the time. Now he states he just wanted to feel better—that's why he's had a relationship outside of their marriage. Mary also confronted this woman and she acted like she was making a big deal out of nothing. There wasn't anything going on she said, and that they were just friends. Yeah right! I've heard that one before. When you're busted, you'll say anything to get out of a tight spot.

Wow, I thought I was at a low point in my life! My situation seems pretty calm compared to hers. I'm telling you, there's just something in the water (or even in the air) around here. As Mary told me what was going on, I got that same gut wrenching feeling I had when I busted my significant other. I don't understand what men are thinking these days. All around me is disaster and despair. I even saw, Rob, a male co-worker of mine, and told him what happened to me. The first thing out of his mouth was, "Are you going to counseling?" This surprised me to hear those words coming out of a guy's mouth. My response was, "If a guy hits me or cheats on me, he's gone!" He still insisted that I could try and save my marriage. I then proceeded to tell him that my significant other wanted to live with her. His immediate reaction was that he was sorry to hear that, and I believed that he was really sincere. Maybe I was in a "men bashing" mood, because it seemed that every man around me was a cheat and a liar. Rob really surprised me and made me think that maybe, perhaps, maybe all men aren't like the one I've been dealing with for almost 19 years. This was a very surprising conversation to me; I want to be with a guy like that who is sincere and supportive. You know a guy who will give you a tissue when you watch a sad movie, and someone who care about me as much as I care about him. A couple needs to have mutual respect for each other in order for a relationship to work.

After he left, my co-worker beside me asked, "Is he married?" Maybe she said it because she heard me say that he's a nice guy. I know he's been divorced, but I don't understand why. Did he have a wife who was too demanding or overbearing? Maybe I'll never know—but maybe someday I will learn the answer if it was meant to be. But at this point, it would be too soon to get serious about anyone. However, I just need a hug and some reassurance to make me feel ok again. Even when we were together, I didn't get respect and compassion from my ex. For a long time now, he never wanted to be with me in a relationship—both physically and emotionally. I yearn for that feeling again. Maybe I'll get a chance to meet someone with whom I'll click with and it will be right this time.

It's Saturday morning, and today is my Parenting Class. Yes, if you have children, and you're getting divorced, the courts make you take a class on parenting—at least in my state. It's one of the prerequisites or stipulations for my final decree. I can't believe it's been three weeks since I "busted" him. Wow, three weeks—time has passed faster than I thought it could. In addition, my friends keep calling to check on me. They're so concerned that he is going to "screw me over" once more by taking advantage of me financially. I hope that doesn't happen. I don't think I can take any more abuse from him—financial or otherwise.

Well, my class started at 9 a.m. this morning at the local library and I got there 20 minutes too early, so I sat in my vehicle and worked on my Sworn Financial Statement. I played around with it and came up with a figure from my total income and expenses. If he doesn't pay me the $500 a month he promised, I'm screwed. After what he said the other day, I'm a little worried. He made some comment that if we did the Child Support Statement with his income, I'd owe him money. I just want to be able to survive and I told him that we both needed to make it financially. He agreed, but can I trust him? All of these things went through my mind as I waited to get inside the door. As the time ticked away, I finished my paperwork and proceeded inside. I sat in the lobby as the instructor opened the door to the room and then she proceeded to set up her materials. After a few minutes, she was ready and everyone proceeded to line up and people got out their $60 in cash to pay the attendance fee. Just think, I've already paid $110 (my portion) of the filing fee and now I have to pay an additional $60 just because he wandered to the other side—this didn't seem fair to me! The next four hours were going to be interesting. I get to have someone lecture me on how to take care of my child, they give me a piece of paper showing my attendance, and then I proceed to the next step. I feel as if I'm on an assembly line; however, this isn't progress. I'm reverting backward!

After registering, I proceeded inside the classroom. I wanted a seat where I could make a quick escape—the end chair was open; thank goodness! At first there were four chairs between the next victim and myself. I thought I'd feel more comfortable there, but as I looked around, I felt frozen. I don't think I'd felt so awkward in a social setting. This was quite uncomfortable for me. Did I really belong here? In addition, did everyone else feel the same way? More answers to questions that I didn't know. I just sat in my chair and kept my eyes forward. After a few more minutes, which felt like hours, all the chairs were eventually filled and the lecture began. She started with asking who here were ok with being in this class, and who was just down right mad they were there. I'm not sure how I felt. I'm not even sure how anyone else felt too—it was so awkward for everyone. I think if we all had a choice, we would all not be here.

As the class proceeded, we watched a video on children's feelings. They are just like ours, and we all go through the same stages of emotions. However, as adults, we have better coping mechanisms than they do. She pointed our attention to the chart at the front of the room. It showed children's ages and the different emotions they possess at each stage. She also advised that due to their fragile emotions, affected by their parents' divorce, each age group could even revert to a "younger" age as they progress in their loss. Next, we even broke up into small groups and there were five ladies in my group. One of the ladies had her mother there for emotional support—she was lucky. I would describe this woman as in her late 30s and dressed in Muslim attire. I think I really admired her for her strength, for her cultures has a "stick-to-itiveness" that's stronger than someone in a different country, such as the United States. After three of us in the group started talking about our demise, her mother got up and gave each of us a hug. She didn't have to do that, but she stressed her belief in God and she must have been his messenger that day. She really stressed how your faith can get you through anything. It was the first time that I had tears in my eyes since that fateful Saturday. I guess I couldn't help it, after seeing another lady tell of her ex taking her two and six year old children for a week at a time and treat her like dirt. Then the other lady who had been separated for a couple of years admitted that her ex doesn't even see his children due to a domestic violence situation. Wow, we all had lost it—there were enough tears for the whole room just in our group. Were we all losers in a game of Parenting 101? We all had a common bond, so maybe that's why we could talk so frankly to each other.

Later in the lecture, the instructor wanted to know how we felt when the decision had been made to split. I blurted out, "betrayed."

One guy said, "guilty"—that made me really go deep into thought. Did he cheat on his wife? Does he feel guilty that his vows failed him somehow? Did his wife cheat because he was never there? These classes really made you think about yourself, your kids and how your emotions can really cause havoc in your life. This process has just started. I have a long way to go to be whole again.

Saturday came and went so quickly, and now Sunday was upon me. It's been three weeks since he moved out. Today, I pick up my son for the week—it's my turn. I first ran a few errands and then called my son. I was on my way, and he was anxiously awaiting my arrival. I had asked him for the house numbers for I really wasn't sure which house it was; although, I was somewhat sure where her house was located. I found it once when I caught him cheating, I'm sure I can find it again! I pulled up along side the curb just after turning the corner, and there it was, his truck parked along the sidewalk. He has a rather large truck, so I knew it wouldn't fit in her garage. This ought to be interesting come winter. He had always "needed" his vehicle parked in the garage so that it would be protected from the elements—snow on his truck should be an interesting conversation at their house. As I pulled slowly to the curb, I looked vicariously for her house numbers, but before I could see them clearly, the door opened and out came my son. His dad wasn't far behind. My son was carrying a box of items not visible from my position, but I could see his face and a few tears that were trying not to fall from his eyes. He was visibly upset and he had a look on his face that made him look like his dog just died. It felt like I was in the power position now—just like my ex was last weekend. I hope this "back and forth" thing gets better. This feeling is breaking all of our hearts—just because one of his extruding body parts followed itself to "greener" pastures.

I am still in awe how one person's position and choices, on an issue, can change so many lives—it's incredible. He has upset so many family members just by choosing a person who he thinks can come into his life and fulfill his unyielding needs. I really wonder about his decision. He even told me on Friday that he hasn't even unpacked yet. What does that tell me? Sounds like he's not staying very long. But I don't want him back—are you kidding me? One of my reasons is that I had a friend tell me just the other day how he used to talk really bad behind my back. How can someone take their significant other back into their lives when they do that to them? The verbal and the emotional abuse I endured for years from him and now the adultery factor—I'd be a fool to even consider him back into my home; let alone my life!

Now I can come and go as I please when my son is with him. I can change anything in the house and not get yelled at—as I had before. There is peace in this two-story home now. But, I guess it's not the same over there. My son has mentioned how noisy it is over there. The train tracks are very close, so when his dad tries to take a nap, he is having trouble staying asleep due to the horns and rumble from the trains. I remember when my ex tried to take a nap in this house. He would often complain how the kids behind our house used to play basketball and how much noise they made. Gee, which is noisier…a train or the thump of a basketball on the pavement? That man will never be happy! He's also got a few more things to deal with—his new chick, her daughters, and then all of their friends that come by. He once told me that he was glad that we had a son because girls are so dramatic and can be such "divas." Has he gotten what he has asked for? Who knows? It just seems like his world has changed so dramatically and not for the better—which probably gives me a little bit of satisfaction. The grass isn't always greener on the other side. I just hope that if this relationship doesn't last that he doesn't ask me to go back into his life. I'd be a damned fool to want his ass back in my new bed!

I've already told my girlfriends they have permission to smack me silly if I ever had one thought about him coming back into my life. If it doesn't work out for them, I could just see his dad moving into his friend's house—the one who's been divorced twice and hates women in general? Gee, who's the adult here? As for my son, he needs stability, which is probably why I don't want to move anywhere any time soon.

As we left, it took about 10 minutes for him to become comfortable with me again. But the look on my ex's face said it all as we drove away. His heart was finally pulled away from his chest, and his face showed the sadness of loss. His son was now with his mother for the next week and he had no say in my decision making process. I felt somewhat powerful, but somewhat distraught by the whole event. I knew my son needed some comfort, so we stopped and got him a Coca-Cola, made in Mexico, from a neighborhood restaurant. It was something he had a while back and he said they tasted better than the ones made in the U.S., so it was a treat for him. After he went inside to get one and then returned to my vehicle, I could see the calm in his being once again. We then proceeded home to make some lunch and as we sat outside on the deck, we talked some. I'm not sure if he knew what to say; this was all so new to him, and small talk was the topic of discussion. Afterwards, he proceeded to get his guinea pigs and hang out with them in his room. He was there for pretty much the rest of the day. Maybe he wanted some peace and quiet. Maybe he felt he needed some alone time. It seemed to last several hours, and then he came to talk to me. I didn't know what to do either—this is all new to me too. Both of our routines have been dramatically changed—it's all new for the both of us.

Today, Monday, I talked to my ex and now we can finally meet this Friday afternoon to get more divorce paperwork done. Waiting on him was the one thing that drove me crazy. My theory was that if something needed to be done—just do it! Quit waiting—just get things accomplished now. He always waited until the last minute to do anything. Finally, after this is over, I don't have to be bothered with a man who procrastinates. If the shoe was on the other foot, however, he always wanted me to get it done quickly because he couldn't wait! Respect for women was definitely not in his vocabulary—at least not with his sister, his mother and me.

We do, however, agree for the most part about our son. He comes first, when it comes to his needs. He is very important to us both and we want him to succeed. Although, it did seem strange when he came back home this week. I was a little torn. I like having my freedom and since I don't have the "mom" role 24/7, it is very strange to me. I had always put him first before me, and now I can do what I want when he isn't there. I mean ever since my son was born, I've done 99 percent of everything for him. Did I feel totally responsible for his well-being? I think I did. I even had a job that was 55 miles one way when he was little. The round trip was 110 miles plus (if I had errands to run after work). This job lasted five years, and when I wanted to move closer to my job so that our son could attend Kindergarten closer to where I was working, he had a cow! My ex didn't want to move from his "dream house." He didn't want to negotiate how our son would come and go from school, and he wasn't going to be interrupted in his day to do this chore. So, I got blamed for this too; it was my entire fault once again for disrupting his life. So, to accommodate him when we did get the house sold, I even let him pick out the house we would buy, because I didn't want to hear that, once again, I was ruining his life. But, of course, he wasn't happy about this entire situation. Years later he said that he didn't pick out this house, it wasn't his idea to move here—in the "PUD," as he called it. Now he lives with her in a house with two teenage females near a train track. Go figure? How long will that last? I've said it before—he is a creature of habit and sooner, not later, his natural position will take over and he will start "dating life" again. Why didn't I listen to all of his friends long ago when they asked me how I could stand him? There were so many hints over the years that told me to leave. I guess it was just easier to turn a blind eye.

CHAPTER 6 –

The Darkness All Around Me

*L*ately it seems that every time I turn on the TV, I see a show about infidelity. Tonight was no exception— T*he Diary of a Mad Black Woman* is on TV. If you compare her situation to mine, hers is a lot worse. Her husband literary threw her out the door. He had a moving van packed with her things, and another woman's clothes in her closet when she got home. This man really has nerve! Even though I've seen this movie before my dilemma, I was totally moved by it once again. His callus actions were more than I could imagine. He has such a power position and he uses it to his advantage; especially when it comes to what he wants. What a total jerk—if you haven't seen this movie, I highly recommend it. This show is somewhat unique in its story line; but it's really hitting home now.

As each day comes and goes, I am seeing things differently. I like my new kitchen, my privacy, and how clean the house is all the time. Besides, I'm nobody's maid now either! I am more independent, but I feel scared about my financial situation. I have a secure job, I hope, and in this economy of 2009, a secure job is worth its weight in gold. I am seeing things in a different light too. For example, I had a nice thing happen to me this morning. I went to the grocery store before work and since I am a disabled vet with a knee issue, the handicap spot allows me to park close. After I made my purchase, I proceeded to my vehicle. As I got in and put on my seatbelt, I saw a nicely dressed gentleman, probably in his late 50s walk by. He seemed to be curious about why I had parked there. He must have looked down at my license plate, and as he looked up, a faint smile crossed his face. I'm not sure what he was thinking at the time, but I smiled back. Several thoughts went through my mind. Was he proud I was a veteran? Was he smiling at me because he liked what he saw? Or, was he being respectful because I was a woman? Whatever the reason he had, I felt a sense of security. I actually felt proud of myself for being strong in my situation. Maybe it was God who sent me an angel to just smile upon me this morning and make me feel safe. Whatever or whoever it was, I felt sheltered for just a brief second.

At that moment, I felt that perhaps I could win the heart of a strong, protective man who respected me as I would he. But, where do I meet someone without a lot of baggage who won't drag me down? I have felt so alone for so long, I don't know where to begin again. Maybe I should find a church to attend that could give me the guidance I so desperately need. He was so anti-church "anything" that I didn't attend church for a long time. I can't do that anymore. I'm finally becoming free from his bond. Wow! Did I just say that? What do I do first besides the kitchen cabinets? My next plan has to take shape soon. But I'm taking a break this week in my extra-curricular activities since my son is with me, and since he thinks I'm "ruining" everything around this house.

It's Wednesday; the day for my son's dad to pick him up for dinner. I stopped first at my son's grandma's house to say hello. After about 10 minutes, I was gone and at my house. I fixed a burger and sat to watch TV. It was weird; I wanted to do something like start on the bathroom cabinets, but I refrained. I resorted to sweeping out the garage. I guess I had to keep myself busy; I've never been so out of sorts like this before. It was soon 7:30 p.m. and I thought I'd call my son. He and his dad just happened to be ready to leave her house, and I had asked my ex to see if he could fix the garbage disposal when he got here. Something happened when I cleaned out the fish tank and now that stupid thing didn't work. It seemed so trivial, and that was what he was good at—

fixing little things. He didn't have any sense of obligation to fix anything around here now, but he did agree to look at it when they arrived. It was just minutes after he fixed it that I had a sense of relief again. But was I really relieved? I almost felt obligated to him; he had always been around to "fix" things—he was really handy at that kind of thing. I guess, "I am woman, hear me roar," didn't apply in this situation. Afterwards, we went into the garage and actually talked to each other in a calm voice and it felt like we had never argued about anything in our entire married life. Go figure? Although, I have a feeling one big argument is just around the corner. This man who hadn't given me the time of day for a very long time actually wanted to have an informative conversation with me this evening. It's almost like a cat that is nice to you one minute, and the next they are ready to strike. No wonder my sense of caution is so awake and alive when I'm around him.

Should I still be mad at him for all of his deceit? Part of me wants to forgive him, but the other half wants to pounce on him and smack the crap out of his being! He hurt me like no other man had before. He took our vows and crumpled them like rice paper. His respect for our marriage is now null and void. My whole way of being has changed just because of his decisions. Should I thank him for giving me my freedom back? I'm torn. Although I am getting back into a routine and my focus for the most part is the way it was, I'm doing things differently now. I'm eating less food but better food. I've lost 10 pounds, and I don't crave what I once did. I'm more aware of the people around me and I see them differently. I notice men more; maybe I'm checking them out—I never did that when I was married. I mean, really married!

Perhaps I'm looking for a love interest; I don't know at this point in my life. Confusion is the name of the game right now. Before, when I was "married," I didn't have wandering eyes even though I was obviously miserable for a very long time. I wasn't raised that way—my morals were a definite part of me, and I respected them. So, why did he wander? I could come up with a million reasons, but would they all be correct? Maybe, I'll never know.

It's been two days since I entered anything into this journal. Maybe that's why I couldn't sleep last night. It must have been around 2:30 a.m. when I woke up and couldn't get back to sleep. I kept thinking about the events of yesterday. I got together with him to get more paperwork done. It took almost four hours to complete all of the documents. Why couldn't I get him to do this sooner? I guess everything was on "his" time. Why couldn't we just do things when we weren't in a hurry to complete them? It seemed like everything was always in a rush where he was concerned. I liked to do things in a manner where it was comfortable; his idea was different. He always waited to do things in the last minute—at least it was that way with me. I was always used to planning and doing things where I wasn't rushed. I'd even get to work a little early—he always told me that since I only worked 10 minutes away, I should leave exactly 10 minutes before I had to be there. I mean yesterday was the perfect example. I had left for work around 7 a.m. and got only down the street when I realized I had a flat tire. After calling my roadside assistance service, I had a landscaper stop and help me, and although they arrived several minutes later, the landscaper had almost completed the tire change before this guy had gotten there. The first gentleman asked for nothing, but assumed that I was in distress and stopped to help me. The other guy just watched to make sure everything was done correctly. I felt so secure knowing that there were men out there to help a woman in need, but didn't ask for anything in return. This blip in my day caused me to get to work almost an hour late, and I was calm about the whole situation. Now, if that had happened to him, he would have been frazzled for the rest of the day. But, for me, I plan for things that could happen. He doesn't think bad things can happen as often as they do, so he then proceeds to fall apart afterwards when they don't go as he had planned. It's like how I view driving a vehicle. I assume everyone around me can't drive, so it makes me a better driver since I don't trust anyone's actions. I mean, what would he have done if someone had stopped and helped him change a tire?

After arriving at work, I was so appreciative that I sought out this gentleman from his company sign on his van. After a few phone calls, I finally found his supervisor and I informed him that his employee didn't have to stop and help me but he did. I didn't know his name, but he helped me without my asking and he didn't even accept my money as an offering for his assistance. His supervisor seemed quite pleased that I had sought after some recognition for his employee's actions. Maybe there are angels out there and God takes care of those who believe in him. I just know I was helped in a desperate moment in my life when I needed the help; if only the other things in my life would fall into place as quickly.

Perhaps things are turning around for me and I've just not seen it yet. When I met with my ex yesterday, we joked that now probably one of us would win the lottery since we were getting a divorce. This was probably a thought that money would be the answer to our ills. Boy, are we confused! I think that money can give you a comfortable life style, but it will never solve our marital bliss—no matter how you see it. It could have solved a lot of our debt right now, and gave us a comfortable home to live in, but who wants a comfortable home when your spouse is cheating? It could have also gotten us away from the noisy neighbors behind us. I guess money is just "eye candy" when you want to dream. Personally, I'd like to move into a different home, but reality is a constant reminder that dreams don't always show up when you need them. I also can't move right now because I'd really upset my son—an earthquake has already shaken his world; another move would destroy him. He's so vulnerable to this whole mess.

Another change in the world is that Walter Cronkite died last night, July 17, 2009. It's interesting to see how the world keeps ticking and moving ahead while your own individual world falls apart. If you can't pull yourself up, the world won't wait for you to get your life together. So, why does it seem that I'm moving on so quickly now? Sometimes I don't know the answer, but maybe my background has something to do with my decisions. In my family I was the younger of two children, and a female. I have only one brother, but I saw my parents and him be very laid back and somewhat shy about anything. Maybe I didn't have their patience with the way they did everything. I mean, when my dad bought a new truck back in the early 70s and a few things he had requested weren't there, he just got mad. I told him that I'd write a letter to the company for him. He didn't want me to help him for a few weeks, and he was angry for that entire time frame. He finally relented, and I went to work on a letter that would get their attention. I wasn't very old—just a teenager, but I was determined to help him through his plight. I worked on that letter for a couple of days, and when I was done, my dad read it and was very surprised. I had said the things he didn't know how to say. He signed it and then it was sent off to the company. I'm not sure if he thought it would do any good or not, but I think he was proud that he was standing up to them. It seemed like a week or two later that my dad got the answer he wanted. Now, he had a credit at the local dealership and could pick out whatever he wanted up to $250. That was a lot of money in the 70s! He was so happy about the results and he immediately went to the dealership and got those big mirrors and a few other things he wanted for his new truck. This was my earliest memory of my strength to not let the "bastards" get me down. I look back at that and it is confirmation to myself that I can make things happen in my life and in the lives of others.

I have often thought about this incident. Maybe I took that and other memories to the point at which I am now. Although I used to be very shy and an introvert in high school, I truly believe that joining the U.S. Navy really brought me out of my shell. Whatever it was, I am thankful, because now I am stronger than I had ever thought I would be. Even on Thursday, when I told my hygienist about my new life, she commented that my one-week of a total meltdown was unusual, because for some people it drags on for months or even years. It had only been a few weeks for me, but I felt so free and relieved. She responded by saying that so many of her clients had sat in the same chair and had told of the same story—she had lost count of her patients and of this same scenario. This disease has to stop!

Today is Saturday—four weeks have lapsed. One month since he left my life—well, at least my house, and I've made so many changes thus far. The kitchen cabinets are done, the family room and kitchen walls have been repainted, and as of today, I have a new member of my household. I went to the animal shelter and got a cat today, along with a few cat toys and food. At first this animal was really spooked—a new place, new everything. Poor thing—he had originally been adopted, but returned to the shelter because he didn't fit in with his new family. Although, after a few hours at my place, he got a bath; that is, after he let me catch him. He wasn't happy with me, but afterwards, I think he felt better. He definitely needed a bath—he was just a little to stinky for me. After he began drying off, he allowed me to brush his fur. He then wanted to hang out upstairs with my son on his bed.

It feels weird having a cat again. When I first met my ex, I had a cat and that was back in 1988—almost 20 years ago. Wow! After we had dated for a few months, and he asked me to marry him, I gave up my precious animal because he was allergic. That should have been my first clue—never give up your pet for your new partner; they must accept your pets or they're gone! I should have known that when he would mess with my cat by rubbing his tail the wrong way, that he would neither respect me, nor my pets. I have learned one thing; however, I will demand that the next man I meet will respect my pets and also me, or he's gone just as fast as I can tell him to make sure the door doesn't hit him in the ass on the way out!

Sunday is now here. It's transition day once again. My son was expecting to go to his dad's house today early. Although, his dad basically said it was more convenient if he come around 3 or 4pm—he had some things to do and he didn't want our son to come any sooner than that time period. There he goes, being selfish again. It's sad to say that his dad is so selfish, but he is that way and probably always will be. As for me, I would drop anything and everything for my son. His dad would say, "give me an hour." Even talking to him today drove me crazy. He wants to split everything 50/50 when it comes to our son, but he says things that contradict himself. He likes to inform me of how much money he's NOT making every month, and now he has two households to carry—Whaah! Give me a break! He also told me that if his business deal comes through by the end of the year, he'll give me a big chunk of money to basically pay me off until our son is 18 years of age—well guess what, it's 19 before child support goes away in this state! He's still confused about life. Well, he is a mortgage broker and he was used to making a lot of money, but this economy is taking a toll on his income. Now he's lucky to make as much as me every month and I'm sure it's taking a toll on his psyche.

He used to brag about how much money he was making, but he surely didn't splurge on me. He was such an ass then. However, he did buy me a 3-stone diamond ring for Christmas once. Although I didn't know it at the time, it was the cheapest ring he could have bought, and then he complained how much he spent on it—why did he bother? He had such a habit of making me feel really small, and insignificant. Besides, lies and deceit, in addition to being cheap, it got easier and easier for him to come up with the next lie. He seemed to practice a lot of this nonsense.

CHAPTER 7 –

Making Changes

now have a new goal; I'm changing my life, and for the better. Today, after I dropped off my son, I bought myself a new coffee table and end table. I financed them, and when I get them paid off, I am going to get a new kitchen table and chairs. I'm so sick of the "cheap" look of the furniture in this home, and little by little, it will change and it will look good. I'm on a mission to erase his memory for good—I roof over my head—I have to in order to survive.

Since we filed our other paperwork on Friday so late, we now have to go to court on Monday morning anyway. Gee, if we had had this stuff done when I wanted, we probably wouldn't have to go tomorrow morning. Great! Another thing I have to do with him!

He keeps driving me crazy—why doesn't he go away for good? I'm feeling a little guilty, because I don't know if I want him to die in a plane crash or have a heart attack! Should I be thinking this way? Who knows? He broke our vows, not me! Some days I want to yell, scream, and even punch him. Other times, I just vent to my friends and co-workers and have these feelings leave my side. Maybe I just want what he has—someone to love me and to be intimate with. I miss the companionship of a guy who really loves me. I want to kiss a guy again who will send shivers down my spine. I want to grow old with my true love—my soul mate. I don't want someone to pretend to love me. I know I've said that I like my time alone, but it's just the cat, two guinea pigs, in addition to the fish in my house and me, and none of them can talk. Although the cat does try to communicate with me, I don't consider "meow" a legible word. I need some male companionship.

With my loneliness in mind, I don't believe what I did last night. I went onto an on-line dating service and put in a profile. Am I ready for something like that? Maybe. Well, on the site, I saw several men, and many of them successful, who are looking to improve their love life, too. It's funny that I wanted to do this—that's how I met my ex originally. At that time, dating services weren't on-line, but profiles were actually mailed to each client. It actually worked for us—or did it? I remember he used to say, "That stuff doesn't work," and then he'd laugh. At that time, he wasn't serious about his words, but maybe here was some truth to that comment. He also used to say, "We've been together all these years, and I can still make you laugh!" Well that used to be true, now he makes me angry, sad, and frustrated. Boy, how times have changed! Now, he makes me wonder why I put up with him for so long. I know I'm not perfect either. I know I pushed a lot of his buttons too. I just wish he would have listened to my needs and wants as well as his own. I know I've said it before, but I wish life wasn't always about him. I really think he got burned so badly when he was younger with various issues, and he never got passed them. I almost, and I stress "almost," feel sorry for him. Why does he take life so seriously? We're only here on earth for such a short time—why make life so miserable for yourself?

It's been two days since I last wrote in this journal. The on-line dating service has been my inspiration, I guess. I now have something to pursue, which is worth the entertaining value for which I paid. I'm really seeing several guys that interest me. I even have one guy who's put me in his "favorites" file. At first, he didn't interest me, but after reading his profile and really thinking about what he said, he really seems like a nice guy. He lives in the next town, which is only about 10 miles away, and I replied to him, so he knew of my interest. I guess this is the first step to meet someone since he showed interest first. I believe he is 49 years old, with salt and pepper hair, and he has a great smile. He says he likes cats. Well that's a first; I'm not giving up my cat this time! People just have to have mutual expectations and mutual interests. Plus, I'm too old, sometimes, to compromise—I'm more cautious now and it will be interesting to find someone at this point in my life. So should I ask him to meet, or should I wait for him? Maybe, I'm a little old fashion; I want him to contact me. Hopefully by this weekend we can meet.

It's Wednesday; dinner with my son again. This time it went ok. It was short, because he wanted to go back to his dad's place early to watch a show with him. He seems to be ok so far with us on our "off" weeks. When I called him today to ask what he wanted for dinner, he seemed to be excited that we were going to be together tonight. Is he settling in now? Does he feel more comfortable with his new situation? I'm not sure if I have an answer to that question. I think I'm getting more used to him being away from me. At first, I wasn't sure, but I have started really enjoying my free time because before I didn't have free time. His dad had the digs on that gold nugget. I guess it's my turn to play "hooky." I'm still on the dating service and tonight I saw a guy who totally intrigued me. I e-mailed him, but only after he showed interest in me first. He's from California—go figure? I'm located a few states away from him, so I'm not sure if a long distance relationship would work. I guess I'm still not used to this dating thing yet. It's been a long time since I even really looked at another man with any interest. The years have taken a toll on both them and me; we've all aged a lot since I was single.

I wish my life now could be reflected in my co-worker, Mary. Her husband is going crazy with this other chick from his company of whom he is fooling around. She's devastated and wondering what to do next. I guess when you get hit with a bat when you don't know it's coming, it throws you for a loop. She did come to a decision today—divorce is definitely the option for her. I guess the most amazing part of this whole thing is that he is talking about her behind her back and has no interest of working anything out with her. What an Ass! They've been together for almost 25 years! Now, he's going through a "mid-life" crisis and taking her down while he's trying to build himself up. Why do men think with that extremity of theirs—you know, that "thing" that has no brain? I guess some men aren't like that, but lately I've seen way too many that do think that way. One day this mystery may be solved, but I doubt it. I don't think God has any miracles for that irritation for women. I guess Hell will have to freeze over when men will have more feelings than brains.

It's another day closer to the weekend, but that is the good news. It was another restless night of not much sleep. I even woke up thinking I heard the doorbell. No, I know I heard it; the attic fan was on, but I still heard something. That's the one thing that spooks me about living alone. Every little noise that arises, I hear it! I don't have any protection; I have a cat. What's he going to do...hiss and then run the other direction? Even though I lock the doors and arm my SUV with its security system, there's always a chance someone could break into my house and harm me. I guess I have to give my ex credit for that—I did feel safer when he was here in this house.

It's been such a long time since I had to fend for myself; I feel like I'm starting from scratch again, just like I was when I was 19 years old. It's scary sometimes. I even had a dream last night that I was riding my bicycle in Washington, D.C., and the longer I rode, the more lost I became. I even passed by a cop but I kept riding. In my dream, I told myself to stop and ask for directions, but I didn't and kept going. Finally, I stopped at an out-of-the-way antique store, but did not ask for directions once more. I soon left and kept riding—I was becoming more and more scared. Right when my heart was racing to its fullest, the alarm clock went off. I quickly woke up and my heart was pounding. My only relief came when I realized it was a dream. I had had this dream a long time ago, so I was familiar with its meaning. My life right now was telling me that I'm treading on uncertain or unfamiliar ground, but I have the stamina to keep going even though I'm unsure of my future. I'm looking forward to upcoming opportunities, but I don't want to go it alone—even though I know I could. This brings me to my co-worker, Mary. She's finally got the courage to say that she's going to file for divorce from her husband. This man, whom she's been with since she was 17 years old, can smile in her face, but has a knife waiting to thrust in her back at any time. However, she had installed a computer program that gave her the ammunition she need to bust both him and this woman. She's also going to inform this lady's significant other of their actions to give him reason to kick her out of their home and send her packing to the curb.

What kind of husband does this to their wife? I've gone through it, and now her! Does he hate her so much that he enjoys her devastation? What a jackass! At least my ex admitted he was having an affair, and moved out immediately. Karma needs to kick him in his backside! With a breakup comes so much frustration and another thing that's such a struggle is finances— I'm wondering about it and so is Mary. I hope her situation gets better soon, so that she can get the strength she needs and the self-confidence she deserves, but currently lacks. I guess these qualities come with past experiences, but since she's been with him for so long, he has had several years to convince her that he was the "man of the house, and she looked up to him. She's admitted to me that she doesn't have any self-confidence at all and she has a lot of negativity in her life. I guess the worst thing about all of our situations is these guys have no clue what they are putting us through. For her, though, it sounds like he's always been in control and takes pride in hurting her. My ex has a control issue too. He always wanted me to go along with him on his ideas—because he was always "right." He had a plan and it would work! Well, guess what? No, it didn't! It wasn't the two of us making decisions together; it was he with his plan of action. Whenever I would disagree with him, he would really be out of sorts; he couldn't see my point of view at all. Why did he always think that his ideas were always correct? Besides, a lot of his ideas failed, and he, for the most part, blamed the actions of others for his demise. Sometimes he was right, but other times, he was totally wrong. It seemed that he couldn't accept that his plan wasn't going to work, and then he had problems accepting full responsibility for the outcome. Therein lies the problem, but not the solution.

It's Saturday again. Lots of things happened yesterday that is worth mentioning. My co-worker, Mary, was monitoring her husband's actions while he was on their computer. The graphic details seemed to get more graphic as the days had progressed this week. Each and every line was enough for her to get physically ill. The mannerisms that were used between them were enough to disgust a teenager. Maybe she had had it and couldn't take it anymore, because her first impulse was to wait until Monday, but she went off the deep end and copied several of their conversations and sent three e-mails. One went to her husband, one to the other woman, and the third went to that woman's significant other. But, before she did that, she called this woman's significant other and told him of her suspicions. He didn't believe her at all, but thought those two were just good friends.

So what happened? Well, the significant other was furious and ready to talk to Mary's husband and I don't mean sitting down having a conversation. His idea of a conversation didn't involve words; well, Mary's husband got scared off and ran like a coward. Mary felt so empowered; I had never seen her feel so confident. I've known her for around a year and her self-confidence is finally starting to bloom. She finally stood up to him after all those years and made a statement in her behalf. I was really proud of her. However, I know she was a little anxious about going home last night because of what she created for him. I was a little worried about her, so I gave her my phone number and told her to call me so I knew she was ok.

She said that she'd call, so I'm hopeful she will. Talk about a love triangle—or in this case a "love battle between four people." It amazes me that the actions of two people, who are still married to their spouses, could cause such chaos! Yeah, I'm there too, but I can keep my head held high because I didn't cheat on my man. I'm sure I could have cheated, but I guess I was quite miserable in my own stew pot and didn't realize it. Also, I guess this chick just bought a new house with her significant other—that's going to be interesting to see what will happen there. I mean, she's 55 years old and Mary's husband is 50. Is the mid-life crisis at the age of 40 or 50 now, or can it happen at any age? Is there any limit at which people commit "stupid?" Maybe we'll never know.

Anyway, as for me, I'm still on the dating website and last evening after I mowed the grass and washed my truck, I checked my account and I had an e-mail! My curiosity was peaked, and after opening it, I had e-mail from the guy who interested me just the day before. When I saw his picture, I was immediately smitten. Then, I read his profile and was really interested. I had sent a response back and asked why didn't he live in Colorado! He lives in California—just a plane ride away! However, long distance relationships are quite hard sometimes. He wanted to know more about me—Wow, that's a first! I haven't had anyone who just wanted to know more about me—wow, I'm shocked! I immediately got to writing him and then sent it off. Maybe I was curious, or I just wanted to see his response, but I had to re-read it, and then I realized that I didn't answer half of his questions. So, I made some notes and then proceeded to give him more information. It was after 9 p.m. last night when I sent out these e-mails, and when I checked my account this morning at 8 a.m. this morning, he hadn't responded yet. Maybe I'm too anxious, but I haven't felt that good about a guy's interest in me in so long that it was quite a compliment.

Maybe I just crave the affection and warmth of a guy who wants to be with me, and that I can reciprocate his affection. There's something to be said for a mate who sends shivers down your spine just by their presence. I don't even remember when my soon to be ex kissed and hugged me—sad, huh? Maybe fanaticizing about a new love interest will make the old, tired and loveless "me" go away. I hope this happens; I really deserve someone too. I hope to get a response from this new guy. He even gave me his name—that's a start, huh? He at least has opened up some. I mean, I need to know why a 50-year-old man has never been married—a little surprising, but not unusual. I mean there are circumstances that could have led to this, but I need to proceed cautiously. Part of me wants to get to know him quickly and the other part is a little scared. I've been so deprived of affection from a guy who wants to be with me, that my heart feels a little starved. I guess there are so many things that go through one's mind when a breakup occurs. I remember years ago at a job that I had where a lady's husband had left her for another man—it was quite a blow for her and she was quite devastated. She was so upset that she slept with every guy she could find to, I guess, get her "womanhood" back. She obviously wanted to prove to herself that she didn't drive her man away. Or was it to prove that she didn't drive her husband to the same sex due to her actions. She ended up getting pregnant, and surprisingly, she did keep her baby.

I couldn't imagine going through that mess. I mean do you prove to yourself that the love of your life, who said they would love you forever and ever, is now telling you he is gay and never wanted to be with you—ever? I don't have anything against people who choose a same-sex partner; it's just a shame that a person couldn't have realized that emotion before they became involved with a person who is straight. I only wish people could be themselves and choose a partner with truth showing through their heart and mind. They shouldn't pretend to be something or someone they're not and this should start from the beginning of a relationship. I guess dealings with others can take a toll on us all and sometimes we get wrapped up in the moment and we all do things that come back to haunt us forever. It seems we all say, "Well if I knew then what I know now, there would have been a lot more changes in our lives." That's the funny part of life, we go through the challenges of day to day things, but we never really know if what we're doing will ultimately lead us to where we want to be in 20 years. It all seems like such a game—one that will test us, eventually.

Sounds like a plan, huh? Maybe I can look back now and see how differently I thought about things when I was in my 20s. Now that I'm in my 40s, life is very different especially in this economy. Plus, retirement is closer than it was before, my son is a teenager, and within five years, he'll be out of high school (I hope). I guess looking forward to your new life after a divorce, is better than looking backwards through that rear-view mirror, even though you have no idea of what your future will hold. Or in my case, he was sewing his wild oats for the second time in his life. Do I feel regret? I'm not sure yet. The pain of what once was, is still lingering, but each day I'm doing a little better.

CHAPTER 8 –

My Comfort Zone

t's Saturday night—is it me or are people worried about me? The only reason I mention this is that a friend, who used to live beside me, along and her husband talked to me this evening about my current situation. In addition, I talked to my mom today who informed me that she would like for me to move "back home." Is she kidding me? I left West Virginia for a reason, and I'm not moving back. I'm happy living in Colorado—I've been here for almost 21 years—longer than I ever lived there. There's no way I could return there and try and make a new life. I understand she's just being a mom and no matter how old you get, your mom is still your mom, and she will protect you no matter what! So, with that in mind, I have an old saying that goes without recognition, "Hell Hath No Furry Like A Pissed Off Mom," and I think she's at that point with my ex.

Each day has given me new challenges—either great days or really crappy days. Well, today was quite boring; perhaps my first mistake was wishing I had something to do. So, I went over to my soon-to-be ex-mother-in- law's house only because her daughter was coming in from out of town today. I thought it was "proper" to at least say hello. I thought I'd pretend to want to see her to keep up appearances. It was hard—things have changed so much since the last time I saw her. Now the time will come that I won't be related to them both. My mother-in-law will now be my son's grandmother. His aunt will still be his aunt; but now I'll have an ex-sister-in-law. This all seems foreign to me. Things sure change when you get divorced—just like they change when you get married. All these relatives and ex-relatives are confusing for everyone. I mean, whom do you still keep in contact with? Do you stay friends with, at least, some of them? Or, do you just drop everyone and hope for the best? Either way you lose. It's a life changing experience for sure. His choices have changed my life totally—is it fair? Probably not. Is it comfortable? Not really. It's almost like death—one minute you're here and the next you're not. But one good thing that I started to do is go back to church. A friend from work invited me to go with her so tomorrow I'm going. I haven't gone in years. I don't even know what to wear. The only thing that I do know is that I have to find myself, or whatever is left of me, and it has to start somehow.

It's Sunday, and I am going to meet my friend at her house and then proceed to church. When we arrived there, I realized how overdressed I was. This church was different; people were wearing blue jeans—something new for me! This non-denominational church was really more comfortable that I had realized; no wonder my friend loved it. The service started with singing and throughout the service, I could feel my eyes filling up with tears. It was the first time that I've been this emotional since the day I found out that my life would change forever. I kept my wits about me during the entire sermon, but after it ended, I just lost it as we walked down the aisle. My friend asked if I wanted to stop and sit for a moment; I agreed. I just had to regroup! At that moment, I just felt like the Noah's flood had appeared once again, and it was taking me back out to sea to drown. I must have looked like I needed therapy, for a lady from the congregation stopped and sat with us for a while. She asked if she could assist, and I just spilled my guts to her and told her that my husband of almost 19 years had an affair and left me. She offered counseling from the church, but I wasn't ready. I didn't feel insulted; I just wasn't ready for an outsider to assist me in anything in my life right now. The pain and grief of the whole situation was too overwhelming, but I think church was what I needed at this time. This was my way to have grief therapy and

111

counseling, but also disappear within a crowd.

After about five minutes, I got it back together, red puffy eyes and all, and we left. I dropped off my friend, and with a hug goodbye, and I was off to my house. I think I cried the next five miles. Why did a church service make me re-live that fateful day? I thought I had it all together—NOT! Obviously, there were residual emotions of a death in my life, and all of those emotions were locked up tight. Maybe I didn't want anyone to go there with me, and if I kept these emotions in Pandora's box, they would never get free. One's mind is quite unique—it seems that if we hide our emotions, or don't talk about them, we can once again regain our control. How confused are we? Well, duh! I fell victim to that one too.

As I returned home, I pulled into my garage and then hit the button to shut the door. I didn't want to get out of my vehicle, but I made myself. It was almost 11:30, and I wanted to shift my emotions into something productive besides tears from my eyes, so I went inside and then started to clean out the filing cabinet in the office. This was something I needed to do forever, but didn't. Now I had an excuse because there was so much stuff that needed to go away—some things several years old that I no longer needed. I even found some items that he should have. So, what did I do? I called to tell him that I found more of his things—but he didn't answer his phone. Once again, this didn't surprise me.

Why should he answer? He doesn't have to pay homage to me anymore—not like he ever did! He has a life that he obviously wants and needs and I'm not included anymore. I even tried to call my son. The same thing happened—he didn't answer either. Why do I bother? But, I knew I would see them both soon, and before long, it was 4 p.m. and I heard my son trying to open the front door—his dad had dropped him off. I unlocked the door to let him in and, of course, his dad had just left, without knowing his son was inside and safe. Was he avoiding me? It seemed like it, but whatever, I saw his priority--himself. What an ass! I had wanted his dad to help me fix the waterbed frame that was falling apart. My son had messed it up so bad by messing with the cat, that it was leaning since the frame fell down. I hated that bed. It was where he slept and I wanted nothing to do with it—I wanted it banished from my house. It was originally a waterbed, but now it had just a mattress lying on the frame and it was lumpy—another piece of crap in my life that needed to go away. I even told my ex that when we bought this mattress that it was too hard. Did he hear me? No! Then, years after we bought it, I mentioned that I didn't want such a hard mattress, and his response was, "Well, I didn't know that!" It was as if he had never heard a word that came out of my mouth. He had his own agenda, and I wasn't part of it. I didn't matter because it was his wants and needs that were set apart of my own. Shameful, huh? This issue started so long ago, and it reiterated to me that I was miserable much sooner than I thought! Right now, I just need a man's arms around me and really tight! I feel so lonely and afraid and I'm scared. I just want God to be close to me, and keep me from harm. I want someone to want me.

Even before my son got home today, I went on my dating service, and there was another guy; this time in South Carolina saying sweet things to me. He hadn't joined the dating service like me, but he saw my profile and said the angels must have sent me to him. He wanted me to e-mail him at work and definitely stay in touch. But, he's far—Colorado and South Carolina are a light world apart. I've e-mailed him anyway and told him of my current situation. What else could I say? He needed to know the truth and where I'm at now in my life. I told him I was separated, and on the healing path. However, my breakdown today doesn't match my response this morning. Maybe I just needed another good cry? Maybe I'm still trying to heal a wound that was opened up by my ex. I don't know. All I do know, though, is that my son came home today and said that his dad kissed "her" in front of him. This really upset him, and the comment made by his dad was that this is a sign of a good relationship. Deep down, I lost it again—more insult to injury—that bastard! How is a good relationship based upon deceit, lies and dishonesty? Maybe I have my head screwed on wrong? The next comment from my son was that they slept in the same bed, and that they probably had sex too! I know this really upset him. This was one more thing for him to grasp around a reality stick. I had to keep the conversation going, so I asked him why it made him so upset, and if it was the fact that his mom and dad weren't kissing, but it was between the two of them? I think he agreed, but he really was done with the conversation and he clammed up again. On this note, I wonder why I was upset—my ex really wasn't a good kisser. Why did this concern me as well? I guess the "first" of everything of his new relationship was going to get to me somehow. Now he had a new "love" and it wasn't me; I was alone now, and had to fend for myself. Maybe it was due to the fact that he did this behind my back and then left after I found out. Perhaps, I felt like a fool for staying with him for so long and after I had suspected his infidelity? I hate him for the emotions that I'm now feeling. How dare he make me feel so sad and alone! If I have any reason to hate him for anything, these are the reasons. Did he think that I was a stone-cold statue without any feelings? Or, was he thinking about himself and only himself and what he wanted—I think so!

My son is caught in the middle of this mess. Then, I made the mistake of telling my son that I might date someone in the future. He wasn't too keen on that idea. I guess he first needs to get used to his dad's situation and all of the changes there. I know he would be mad, but I need to get on with my life too! I don't want to hurt forever, but I can't make him understand that right now. So, with this in mind, why do the innocent get hurt the worst? His actions have caused so much grief in both of our lives—that selfish bastard! I hate him more than I feel sorry for him. My son even said that his dad is even going back to his old habits; which was making his own wine. He stopped doing that a while back when he lived here because he lost interest. I guess everything he once enjoyed and then hated by being with me, he now feels comfortable doing again because he is with her? He's a creature of habit, so now that he's happy again, I guess he wants to do old hobbies once more. Perhaps a change of scenery makes him happy; I guess. That bastard! He's up to his old ways once again. Just wait until she gets tired of his old habits—things will not be as rosy! He will never change; I know him too well. However, she'll probably not be tired of him until it's too late—Whaah! The Honeymoon is just starting?

Well, it was during dinner when I found out about his new habits. Maybe it was too much wine with dinner that made me lose it; maybe it was his old interests that were now new, that got to me. But, I excused myself and went upstairs, and there they were—those old friends of mine—the tears in my eyes that came once again to visit me. Damn it! What's wrong with me? Why am I letting him control me still? I've got to move on. What will happen on September 22? The day the final decree will rear its ugly little head? Am I going to cry then too? I don't want to, but it may happen. I feel so vulnerable at this moment and I'm the one who's trying to keep it together. I guess no one knows about this divorce thing until you go through it—it is such an emotional roller coaster. It's like a death—first you're down, then you're laughing, but then you're crying all within a few minutes. I think death is a lot easier to deal with because you have a ceremony to bury a memory and a body. Too bad we can't do that when you get divorced! I don't think he knows how much he hurt me—but do I really want him to have that power? Well, that would be a big "NO!" Part of me wants him to suffer like I have, and the other half wants him to die a violent death, so "she" can suffer like me. Either way, justice would not be served. However, my mind must continue to heal; it has too.

It's now 8 p.m. on Sunday evening. I've calmed down; no more tears, at least for a few minutes, anyway. As I sit here, I really wonder why this has happened. When and why did he stray? When did he first kiss her, and when did he go all the way and feel guilty, but continued down that path? Where was his justification to screw her for the first time? I mean, they kissed and my son saw it and was totally disgusted. Their excuse was "their relationship" is a good relationship. What? How do you base a relationship on what they did? Do they know where they're headed? Probably to the preacher, if I'm right, or maybe to Hell if I'm wrong. Possibly she will be Wife Number 2? But, I guess, it depends on what you call Number 2, right? Deep down I guess I really wish them well, but I also wish them tragedy. Am I wrong for hating their actions? I don't think so—they are so far from right, that how can they see that these decisions are so wrong? Maybe I'm too moral for my own good. He always told me that I was too honest!

Gee, all my life I have been honest when it came to relationships. I never cheated on a guy in that way. Nonetheless, I guess it was about 20 years back when I was accused of trying to take someone's husband—and twice! The truth of the matter is that it was two different friends, on each occasion who did these actions. I was at the wrong place at the wrong time I guess. I don't have that gene in me. I couldn't put another female in that situation—it just hurts too much. For me, I think, I just need to cry really hard, one more time, because there's so much to this divorce thing. One thing that I have found out is that there is a grieving period you must go through to put this "death" in the grave and make it stay there. But, how long must I go through this? How long will it last, because right now, I'm really done with this pain and agony. Do I need a new relationship to heal faster? Does time heal all wounds, and how long do I have to wait before I'm happy once again? There are too many questions in my brain, and I don't have any answers. I guess the most important question is when will my son accept his new life? Maybe someday the answers will fall into place. I hope so; loneliness and despair are not for me! I really want to feel love again with someone who wants to be with me. God, please make this time sooner than later! It's now Tuesday—no word from any of the guys on the dating service. Did I expect an instant man to fall at my feet? Well, if I did, I was obviously confused! I did e-mail one guy who is a cop and likes cats. That's a new one for me—Mr. Tough Guy with a kitty? The other guy from South Carolina must have gotten scared off. I told him how my soon-to-be ex and I were still married, but "D" day is just around the corner. Maybe I shouldn't tell them anything but what they want to hear? I'm just not that way, because, you know, I have been told I'm too honest. Maybe, that's what he likes in her—you know "dishonesty." When she was just a "friend," my ex told me that she has kept secrets from her ex too. I guess they're both good at one thing—hiding secrets. They must be better at it than me.

As for Mary, she was definitely too trusting with her man, but she really didn't have any reason not to suspect anything until now. She has gotten more strength in the last couple of weeks than I've ever seen before. I guess over the weekend, he had a change of heart. He called her on Saturday crying—yes, I said crying, and apologizing for his actions. Did he have a bolt of lightening suddenly hit him? Only now he knows what he did was wrong? I don't get the mentality of someone who cheats. Does the other person in a relationship need to do research so we can understand their actions? That is the ultimate question, and it may never be answered.

On that note, today was enlightening. Mary said something to me that explained a lot. I had wondered why she hasn't wanted to tell me a lot about her situation. She asked me to excuse myself today while she talked to another co-worker. I wondered why, was a little confused, and perhaps a little hurt that she didn't want me around when she was talking to someone else. I found out later when I asked her a work-related question. She apologized and said that she didn't want me to see her cry. Wow! Does she really think that I'm that strong? Even though I sort of knew about my ex and what he was doing, she found out in an instant. Both situations were tough to take, and I did reiterate that I may seem to be strong, but I lost it at church on Sunday. I also told her that my emotions are up and down—anything can set me off into a world of which I am not familiar, and will probably never make me comfortable inside and out. I mean Mary had a flat tire this morning and she actually got her daughter to bring her significant other to her rescue. To me, that's surprising that he would even do an act so nice. I know my ex would probably help me too, but I really want to do it on my own even if it's harder than I would want to admit.

As for this evening, other emotions have now hit me. My son said that his aunt (his dad's sister) is having a "sleepover" at "her" house tonight. A sleepover? Just another way of telling me that he has his sister on his side. Is this a child's game? I think not. But, how uncomfortable could that be for his aunt? I know that she will be gracious and a well-mannered guest because that's just the way she is around people. She was once a business owner and had to smile in the face of diversity all the time, so she's used to "putting on a face." This is just another step in my world that keeps my existence getting smaller and smaller. Or is it that our friends and "soon-to-be" ex-family members are getting more distant. I know my family is behind me 100 percent, but they live in another state, far away from here, so I'm becoming more and more alone. My only refuge consists of my friends—they're my only allies in this mess. But there's a loneliness that I'm feeling that can't be resolved. My son even told me that his dad's friend, Mike, who has an annual pig roast, would soon be holding it again. So, am I invited? Will she be there with him? Should I not show up because I'm not invited ever again? I'm so sick of asking myself these questions—why am I second-guessing myself? I feel so much like an idiot just because my life and the people around me are changing as each day passes, and I'm still stuck in first gear.

I just remember when Mike and his wife were getting divorced. She had an affair and now it was "her fault" that things were changing. It was so strange to never see her again. Is this going to be me now? Do I show up and then tell them that he cheated on me? Well, then he'll know that we will never be seen together in public because he had wandering body parts. I guess now our friends have a choice—friends with him or new enemies with me. Everything will be different this next year. The first test will be that only my son will be my guest at my birthday dinner. Perhaps my ex-mother-in-law will join us? Or will she blow me off and say she can't take sides? I know I've said it before, but his actions have changed so many lives, it's not even funny. I even have an appointment on Saturday to sell my wedding rings and my 3-stone diamond ring. I probably won't get much for them, but they need to go away—permanently. A little more cash wouldn't hurt my situation either. I want to pay off some bills, so this is my first step.

CHAPTER 9 –

Decision Making 101
The Next Steps in Life

I keep getting advice from friends and co-workers— maybe more than I want right now. They've all advised me to not buy anything until the divorce is final. I guess my situation warrants some more thought on my future decisions. I first wanted to refinance the house into my name, but now I really think that it's probably best to just keep my money in something else because this is one asset that I'm not sure I want to keep. Besides, that money could be making me money somewhere else, and not in a house owned by both of us. Who knows, my future someone could have a house and I may want to dispose of this one? Plus, my neighborhood has changed so much in the last eight years, so why would I want to stay here? Families we once hung out with are now gone; replaced by people who don't even say hello or who are rude. Besides, this place doesn't feel like home anymore. I guess my only reason for being here is that my son is familiar with his surroundings—I don't have any other excuse. Maybe that's why I want to redecorate and remove every piece of furniture that reminds me of him. I just want to start fresh and create a new beginning for myself. I'm sure it upsets my son with so many changes that he's seeing in both of his parent's lives. Am I being selfish in my actions? Do I want something better in my life? Sure I do, and maybe just a little selfishness is seeping in to my life too. This period of my life is so fragile that I need a little self-indulgence. I mean his selfishness got us to this point, right? So, I have to pick up the pieces of my life and go on. In other words, I have to bear the cross, get it to the next platform, and stabilize it in the next location. It's hard to keep my stamina in place. Rest, my friends, and my son are my inspiration to keep going. I can't give up; not right now! Maybe I need a long hot bath—something to relax me so I can refresh and regroup. Besides, this evening my son goes with his dad for dinner; yes, it's Wednesday. I'm still not used to this new routine. How did we get to this point? What are the circumstances that led him to cheat? Still, I have so many questions that remain unanswered, and they keep rolling around in my mind constantly. Every time I think back on things, I saw him hate me more and more. He had issues with everything I did. But, why did he constantly want his way on every issue? Perhaps, I didn't have any patience for his journey in life— but it always seemed to be his way or the highway. I even saw him blame others several times for his misfortune. Business deals and his parents' actions were his biggest hang-ups. He couldn't move on with his failures, because he dwelled on them for years. His sister even asked for advice several times and then never took any of it from him. Even when she was in the middle of her own divorce, she would call him to complain about things, constantly. He said he was tired of that whole situation with her and her husband since she wouldn't listen to him.

So, what would have happened if it were me who cheated? Perhaps it would be him saying those same words that are now coming out of my mouth. He would be furious, and confused; I just know it! I would be the "bad guy," and all of his friends would be on his side badmouthing me. Now, since it was he who cheated, it makes me wonder how his friends feel about his actions. Do they think he's scum because he was the one who strayed? Plus, will I ever hear from any of them again—at least the ones I liked? Some of them I don't ever care to ever talk to again since they were just like him. I guess I put up with a lot, but now everyday seems to be a challenge. Some mornings I really have to put more effort into it than I ever have. That's where prayer comes in—something absolutely necessary in any divorce situation or other tragedy. Even today was a challenge. Maybe it was due to the fact that his sister was with them yesterday. The pit of my stomach felt like it did the day he was busted. I was edgy, and sitting still was out of the question. This emotional roller coaster is driving me crazy once again. He even came over this evening to get our son for dinner. He's actually being more responsible now—but why now? He didn't want to be responsible the whole time our son has been alive. I could count on one hand how many times he changed his son's diapers, and how many times he picked up and dropped him off at daycare. Now he's helping me out, but only on his time. He even looked at that bed upstairs that was broken to see if it could be fixed. Personally, I hate that bed. It was "ours" and I never liked it.

So, here comes another expense. I want to get a new frame and new bedding. I guess a windfall wouldn't hurt right about now. But does money ever solve anything? When I think of winning the lottery, I am reminded of that *Roseanne* episode when Roseanne and Dan won the lottery, and they thought their lives would become better. But, that relationship ended up in divorce because he cheated on her; so, I guess wishing upon a star doesn't give you what you want.

Maybe, I'll never know why he strayed, but will it matter in five years? I guess not. Will I be happier after I have the divorce papers in my hand? Well, I may be shocked, saddened, and lost, or I may jump for joy. My future is so uncertain now, but wide open at the same time. There are so many issues to resolve now. Besides, when I talked to Mary today, she said something that I've felt all along—loneliness is now very real. Maybe that's the feeling in the pit of my stomach. I even heard that a manager at work today will be dealing with the state's budget crisis and who knows what will happen to jobs and perhaps layoffs. I hope that doesn't happen—I'd be up a creek if I got laid off. I'm so scared now and the only thing I crave is to have a guy to give me a big hug and a warm smile to tell me everything will work out. Or, gee, perhaps I could live with the happy couple if I got laid off? I think not!

That scared feeling is in the pit of my stomach today. But, I don't feel so desperate to meet anyone through my dating service. I reviewed it last night and took everyone off but the guys who viewed me. I had gotten e-mail from one guy who said, after seeing my picture that our lifestyles were different and the physical attraction wasn't there. I had my doubts at first but had e-mailed him anyway. Some of his pictures showed him going bald, and some of the profile that he had written about himself should have been a red flag. He basically said, "Do me the courtesy of a picture, as I did." He sounds a little conceited if you ask me. I'm better off without someone like that! This time, I will review every little detail about a man and see if he fits my criteria. Don't get me wrong; I'm not unyielding. I just want better for myself this time. I don't like to fight with my significant other; I will have higher expectations this time around. I just want to live a life with someone who is understanding and wants to work things out together.

Today we met with our investment counselor after work. I thought we were first going to split only our investments that we have together. He wanted to add my retirement account to the mix; even though he didn't have one. I just about lost it; I know my reaction was very plain to see. Stopping in my tracks was a knee jerk reaction that surprised even myself. Maybe I wanted more out of this because he was the one who threw our vows in the toilet. Perhaps I wanted him to suffer just a bit more than I was suffering. But in the end, I agreed to a 50/50 split—I just needed another part of my life finished when it came to him. Sometimes it would be easier if he just died before this divorce thing is over. Of course, then my son would suffer. I, on the other hand, would have more money and more closure. I guess I just can't get off this "go away for good" thing.

We even discussed the equity in the house. The original suggestion was to split the equity minus the first and second mortgages from the beginning. Well, I don't want to move yet, and

I'm not buying him out either. There's so much that has to be done with his house that I will be keeping receipts for things that need to be done. Just one more emotional issue—one more thing to negotiate with "him. I was so glad we finished this "meeting," then I went to pick up my son. Of course, I had to hear about how my sister-in-law was visiting the new chick. I guess the "sleepover" was a success. Perhaps, I was still mad at my ex from this meeting, because I caught myself making a comment to his mom that she may have a new daughter-in-law soon. Her response was, "Do you really think so?" My reply was, "Could be?" There it was, the seed was planted. I'm sure that conversation will be relayed to her daughter.

What a trying day! The bottom of my soul hurts. I even had to apologize to our Investor. He knows why we are splitting. He's been there too so he knows my state of mind. He seems so calm now. But I bet when it was his turn; he lost it more than once. I did find out that he slept with more than one woman and for a long while after the fact. I don't get it; I was so calm about a week ago, now I'm an emotional wreck. The hatred in my heart is so profound at this moment that I could scream. But, I've got to keep my self-control—my son is upstairs at this moment. My emotional state needs to chill; I have to use my anger for something positive. I just have to find that outlet. I even talked to my son this evening. He's confused about what a "real relationship" means. I tried to tell him it's based on trust and respect. Maybe our conversation got too deep when I said his dad and his new girlfriend's relationship didn't start out that way. There was a lot of distrust and sneaking around that made me upset and sad. I want to tell him about this, but I have to put it in words that he can understand. He's a teenager and with that goes several different feelings and a lot of confusion. Being a teenager is hard enough, but then add the fact that your dad is a liar and a cheat! He almost got mad and the tears were in the background, but they never materialized this evening. I felt so sorry for him and ashamed for his dad's actions. This is a great way for him to grow up! Where is his male role model when he needs one to look up to? My son has better values than his dad, already, and he's not even in high school. One day, my son will tell his dad his feelings and the shame will be evident to everyone present.

Mary also has teenage sons to educate about their dad. Her oldest son is very vocal about his dad's actions in her whole mess. The younger boy is saying hardly anything, and she is worried that he cannot express himself yet. Another co-worker of mine went through a divorce about a year ago and her son who was 12 at the time did the same thing, but one day he just got angry and expressed his distaste verbally. She wasn't ready when it happened, and she was surprised when it occurred. She just wanted to hold him until the pain went away. But, how do you tell your child that one of their parents has no values when it comes to marriage? The trust factor is gone; the faith and security of a relationship is shaken—perhaps forever? Where are the answers? I guess only time will tell. I want my son to believe in good relationships, and what they can mean for his future.

It's Friday, the day before the weekend. Today, Mary came in late. I thought she was going to file for divorce today, but alas, she only did some errands. She said she was going to wait. She's still giving it some thought. I guess she's trying to find out some answers like me. I already know she can't remove him from her health insurance policy and from the car insurance unless there's a final divorce decree starring her in the face. Boy, you can't get rid of them as fast as you want! You even have to wait 90 days in Colorado to even to have the divorce finalized when you have minor children. This happens only if you agree to everything. Maybe today was one day later than the last, but one more day closer to the end of my "former" life. My stomach is still messed up. That gut wrenching feeling is still there. I even took my son out to eat this evening, but I couldn't eat much. Just a salad and a small bowl of soup were too much. The soup was enough in addition to bottled water. God, will this "sick" feeling ever go away? I'm even losing inches in my hips and waist. My body is shrinking—Good! At least something positive in my life is happening, but, boy, what a way to lose weight! I've always wondered how women could lose so much weight and look so good during a divorce. I guess I know now, but I don't recommend it. I guess it's because they're literally sickened with "divorce syndrome." No sleep and very little food intake really takes its toll on your body. Maybe I'll feel better tomorrow after I sell those useless rings he gave me. They can't be worth much—he was too cheap to buy me anything too nice.

Well, today is Saturday. I have several errands to run including the "ring" thing. My son always looks forward to going with me because he likes to be busy and do things on the weekend. As we completed each chore, we tried to kill some time before we went to the jewelers. At one point, we stopped at a craft store and my son blurted out the fact that he and his dad had gone to Kansas just one week before. Well, I knew they had gone, but his next comment floored me. He stated that they used "her" SUV to drive there and back. When I heard this, those old emotions came flooding back and more questions came to me. How many trips did he take in the past and did she go with him? I mean he went on several business trips and a few vacation trips, all without me, and at this moment I wanted answers. How dare he do this to me! This was just one more thing for me to wonder about and question. How many times were they together when he said he was playing poker with the guys? How dare he make me the fool in their games? Bitterness and loneliness engulfed me once again as I tried to regain my composure. I had more four-letter words for him and several ones that were a little longer just hanging on my tongue just wanting to get out.

Before this conversation began, my son and I were chatting and he said, "I don't trust him." My reaction was, "Who?" although I had a theory on whom he was speaking. He replied, "Dad, because he lied." My heart just sank and my stomach felt sick. How could one person's selfishness cause so much heartache to so many people? I guess his sister was correct when she called him "selfish" so long ago. When I told him that comment, he replied that she was "greedy." It doesn't make sense to me how two siblings could be so alike, and want more for themselves than they give to another. I don't get it. Maybe I don't understand why people act this way and it was hard to talk to my son about any of this. So, when I had stopped later to have my son run into a fast food restaurant to get himself lunch, I tried to call some girlfriends to talk, none were available. Suddenly, that "loneliness" gene snuck up from behind—again—and tore through me like a lightening bolt. This feeling is driving me crazy. It's too hard after being with someone for so many years, and then suddenly I'm going it alone again. Besides, this dating service is only a minor distraction for the moment. Plus, I live in a "family-oriented" housing area. Do I even fit in here anymore? I even contacted a realtor yesterday and got the loan process started. Should

I stay here? Should I move into a condo? There are so many questions, but so few answers. Should I even continue to go to church? I mean, I really need to be with people and get out of my house—these walls have a way of caving in on you when you least expect it. Where is the strength to go on when I need it? I even thought I would get more for my gold rings than I did—all I got was $75. The salesman even told me that the diamonds in the three-stone ring weren't very good quality. I knew it, even before I opened the door to this place.

It just goes to show you that he really was cheap with anything he bought me, but as for him, the sky was the limit. I even found out that he's taking her to Salt Lake City in August when he goes on a business trip. He always told me that I was too high maintenance because I took enough clothes for each day of a trip. He always re-wore his clothes even though they smelled! Besides, I carried my own weight by packing and carrying all of my suitcases, since he refused to help me in any way. What an ass! Selfishness is definitely his first name and not his middle one! Maybe I'll get strength again when a guy pays me the attention I need to feel good about myself. I hope it comes before I lose my mind; I can't take too much more of these ups and down. I'm beginning to know what a manic-depressive person feels like.

It's Sunday; my second weekend at church. Today I had my son so I took him with me. Today the tears still came, but not as bad as last week. At first there was singing, so of course my son was bored until it was time for him to go to the junior high room. But minutes later, he left and the sermon began. It was definitely meant for me today. The Pastor spoke of forgiveness and thirsting for something you think you want. The example he used was wives leaving their husbands, and vice versa. It was almost like he asked my ex for an input into this week's sermon because he needed to know how that felt! This definitely got my attention because I've never heard it put quite so vividly, but boy was he right on target! Where did the Pastor get his inspiration from today? It was quite strange to hear his sermon, but it was definitely meant for me. I even felt a message in my heart that told me to forgive my ex for his decisions—Wow! Does God know what he's asking me to do? This may take a little bit of time to achieve that tremendous task! However, I guess the only way to move on with my life without him is forgiveness. For the rest of my life, I guess I will have questions about what went on, but do I really need to have those answers resolved before I really forgive him? I'm trying really hard to just not think about it, but it's really hard right now. There's just too many emotions for me to sort out; I hope that time will heal my heart.

As I look back there were so many times and excuses that made my ex and my son go over to her house. Did he try to make it ok by taking our son? Was he preparing him for what was to come? What was he thinking? Maybe I'll never figure out why, but do I really want that answer too? All I know is that I have to forgive him or I will never be allowed to move on with my life, and he will still have that control over me. Today has got to be the first step in my process to move forward. I can only pray that Mary can begin the process too. She's a few years younger than me, so when she finally gets her life together and begins the healing process, she'll be ok.

Sunday, today, was interesting when my ex came to get our son. He wanted the drafting board that I had bought several years ago so we could plan out our "dream house." Could they be building a new place together? That's why we had it. I just know that the house they're in now won't due. He can't stand noise and crowds and that describes exactly their situation. They're near a train track and a firehouse, so the noise "effect" is definitely there. Also, my emotions that I thought were gone have come flooding back once more and I feel I'm back at Day 1. That same word came back to haunt me about him—selfishness! I guess it wouldn't be so bad if I had someone new in my life—maybe that's why I feel so alone. Don't get me wrong, I'm really a strong person, I just don't want to have that "lonely" gene imbedded into my skin.

Throughout this time in my life, I've mostly been depressed and lonely, but today I even saw something on TV that made me laugh. It was a story about a man who made a bad decision when it comes to women. This guy was married and also had three mistresses. Well, they all caught up to him and therefore his demise began. All of them found out about each other and then plotted his fate. They basically attacked him and super glued his manhood to his stomach and then left with his wallet, his car and some other things. Just think of the power those women must have taken back, however, it didn't last long, they got busted and were charged with misdemeanor offenses. I probably would have done the same thing, and taken the consequences. It made for a good story line, though. I mean, really, do men think they can get away with this crap? If not in this life, will their next life be their downfall?

I want so much to move on—today, we liquidated our investments. So, I get the cash; he gets the investment that he can't touch without a penalty. At least I get something, and I use the term loosely, out of this marriage. It's not a lot, but I'm not destitute. I'm not really sure what or how to invest it, because he always took care of that part. Guess what? Now, I have one more thing to think about, and I'm scared once again. I can't make a decision too quickly, or it may come back to haunt me. I'll figure out something; now all of the decisions are mine once more. I'm going to be single again, but this time, I'm a "divorcee." That word just sounds wrong. It almost sounds like failure, but on whose part? You know the old saying, "It takes two," but in this case it was three.

As for Mary, she told me that her husband came back for three days, then she kicked him to the curb, again—hopefully, for good this time. When they were out this weekend together, she told him she loved him and then kissed him. His response was, "You don't have to say that all the time!" In addition, he was mad that she told her adult daughters what had happened and what their father had done. Ok, what about this picture doesn't sound right? He cheated on her and then he was mad at Mary for letting her kids know about it! Did he not realize that his actions have consequences? "Should any person realize that? Hello? Is anyone home? I mean the same goes for a woman who pulls the same crap—this street goes two ways!

Another co-worker upstairs, Jane, who has been married for only a short time is also having issues. Apparently he likes to drink, a lot, and it's like she has a child to take care of instead of a life partner. Geez, it seems there are too many men out there wanting "greener grass," than what they have at home. It's like an epidemic of an incurable flu strand—it never goes away. The hope is that we will all survive this crisis happening around us. Will we enjoy life now? I guess the jury is out on that verdict, but there still may be hope. After thinking about what I should do next, I then ran into a friend, who is in her 60s and she's been divorced twice. She is totally enjoying life because she stays busy. She said that now is the time to do all of the things that I never got a chance to do while I was married. I've been trying to do that since it happened to me, and so far it's happening. I've just got to convince Mary that this would be the start of her independence. Jane, another co-worker, is just beginning the second round of divorce number two. I know this woman; she's a kind, compassionate person with hardly a harsh word from her mouth. Unfortunately, she attracts bums into her life, but she only sees their true colors after she says, "I do." I'm just glad she's getting out of her personal prison before she makes herself miserable for a very long time.

In addition to my co-workers and their current situations, my neighbor, Linda, whom I talked with over the weekend, is getting more and more miserable. Life for her is becoming more discontented. Her significant other is not helping with housework, and just being a bum, or continuing on the alcoholism path. Her kids won't even help with anything around the house either. She's sick of picking up after everyone, and playing nanny and or maid to everyone. She's so ready to make a change in her life, but too scared or unsure how to pursue with that change. It seems that everyone around me, who is in this "crisis" mode, has things going on that is the same as mine but in a different way. Some are staying in their marriage for the kids; others stay due to financial reasons. There's never a really good timeframe for a decision to be made. Look at me—it was at least two years ago when I knew my marriage was in the toilet. But, I stayed, why? Maybe it was uncertainty that led me down that same path I had been before because it was familiar and I didn't want to rock the boat. I even dreamt about two years ago how my life would be different if he wasn't in the picture. Was it wishful thinking? Who knows, but it was a nice dream, nevertheless. I just know now that I must pursue my life as I see fit.

The loneliness in my life is quite real at this moment, or is it the fact that my imagination is going a little crazy? The reason I say that is due to the fact that I couldn't sleep last night—once again! I woke up just before 3 a.m. this morning. I turned on the TV for about 30 minutes, which usually helps me get my mind off whatever I'm thinking about, and I can drift off again. Well it was after I hit the pillow again that I had a dream that was so real. I was with my ex, in bed, and we were having relations, if you know what I mean. I just remember wondering what "she" would think if she found out. When I told my co-worker the next day, she told me that I obviously needed some of "that stuff" to get it off my mind. Is my mind really thinking that I'm that hard up? Or, does it just mean that I want someone in my life to constitute a meaningful relationship?

With intimacy in mind, I also talked to my ex today; he mentioned that he put his arm around his new girlfriend, and our son just lost it. He yelled at his dad and told him that he was ashamed of him, and maybe he would go to his Mom's house and live permanently! Wow! I know that teenagers are emotional, but I guess in a divorce situation, times it by 1,000 and you'll get a more visible result. In this case, there was a terribly emotional result. My heart goes out to him. I'm just glad I didn't have any more children with that man! My son even told me on the phone today that he cried last night. Well, I know why, but I acted as if I didn't since his dad had told me this story first. So, I asked him why and I got the standard answer, "I don't know." I told him we would talk more tonight on his thoughts and feelings—he agreed.

After talking to my ex this evening he mentioned that the way our son is acting is due to the fact that he really hasn't been around a "real" relationship before. He obviously only saw one that included fighting and tension. Basically, he was saying our relationship wasn't a good one, but now our son is seeing what a relationship should be! Is this man on drugs? Should I be upset and smack the crap out of him? At this point I don't know. But all I do know is that he still doesn't get it! Gee, does it matter that he ripped our marriage apart because he wanted to screw around behind my back instead of just leaving first? His actions were

141

hurtful to not only his immediate family, but to me and my son. If he just left us, without immediately moving into her house, it could have been different. But, no, he had to lie and cheat until I was miserable to the point of exhaustion in this relationship. Sure we fought, probably because we were both miserable. Now my son sees her as the enemy—the one who broke up his parents. She's not a friend to me anymore; her title is "mistress." In addition, my son has no respect for them both and feels his dad is now a liar. How do you convince him otherwise? Besides, why would I want to try?

My life has flown by these past few weeks, and I can't keep up with anything. My son and I had dinner tonight. It's Wednesday; the day of the week I get to see him when it's my week without him. Tonight my son confessed to me another lie that his dad told him to tell me. He said that when they would spend the whole day together, they would be at her house. Then his dad would tell him that, "Mom doesn't need to know everything we do," and on that note his dad told him to tell me that they were at his dad's friend's house all day. Now, looking back they said that same line a lot. How many more lies can there be? He not only told me lies, but had our son cover his ass too! I don't think I want to know anymore, because the more I know, the more the hatred is present in my heart and it doesn't want to go away. I'm even having trouble believing him about the house, "our" house we lived in; you know, the one where I currently live. He's on the mortgage, and I'm on the Deed of Trust, so I have a vested interest in it. I mean, he could sell it out from under me and I'd be screwed and not have a place to live. Or, if I got a little vindictive, I could just not pay the mortgage and he'd be on the hook. If this gets nasty, we could really hate each other really fast. I hope it doesn't get to that point.

He has offered to do me a favor, however, since he used to be in the mortgage business, he said he would look over the paperwork to see what another lender could offer me. So, after looking into my paperwork, he said that the guy was charging me too much in closing costs for the loan for which I was applying. Then he throws a bomb shell on me—the second on the house that he said he would take care of, well, now he's not in a "position" to pay it off. Well, now I can't afford to buy this house— or do I really want to? At this point, I don't know. I feel like I'm just in a rental. It's no longer my home; maybe it never was meant to be mine? A long time ago, we had a person perform Feng Shui on this home so that we could arrange the contents and colors so it would be soothing. I should have known that when she was performing the "ceremony" and she then spilled the candle wax on the good rug and burned a hole in it, that we didn't belong in this house, either together or separately. The only thing good that happened today in the news was that two journalists were released from North Korea and finally arrived home. Family is important, well at least to a chosen few.

Today my emotions are riding high again. My son is my whole world and he is definitely rocking it. I can take these emotional ups and downs with my ex, but now my son is continuing my saga. My world is so upside down right now and one of my girlfriends, Marie, has heard so much of my dilemma that I think she's worried about me. We are meeting tonight for drinks. I warned her what happened last night, so she's aware of my mood. I'm just glad she's there for me. I've known her for almost 13 years and we've been through a lot together. She's a solid rock when I need a place to set down my troubles and keep them in place. We met after work and, of course, she had to get stuck in traffic, but I called her when I arrived at the restaurant and we chatted until she arrived about 30 minutes later. We were at the restaurant from 5 p.m. until almost 7 p.m. I think we talked about things that we never talked about before. She learned things about me that she never knew and likewise about her. It's strange that people who have known each other for over a decade would know each other better. I guess it's the same in relationships—you can never really know a person and before its too late, you're going down a path of disaster until the "D" word hits you and tears apart your family in every way, shape, and form.

She's a great friend—always there for me and she sometimes thinks about me when she doesn't even know I need her. I don't think I could have made it through this mess without her. In addition, my co-workers, friends, and church have helped me tremendously. Renewing my faith has given me new direction and the strength to overcome my frustrations and to live life to the fullest. I've even decided to go to the mountains soon to go gambling. I've wanted to do that for a long time, but I never could; now is my chance to do what I want without that "anchor" in my life. I hate to admit it, but I've always been "Mom—The Provider." You know, that person who was always there for my son with every meal that was made, every lunch sack filled, and the homework tutor. On the other hand, "he" was always going and doing the things he wanted to do like hunting and fishing trips, short jaunts to the mountains, and everywhere else he decided that I shouldn't go with him. He always made me feel that I was not allowed to do anything for myself—maybe I felt stuck and that's why I always watched TV as much as I did. I never felt like I could take an opportunity to have as much fun as he. Now, I have no overwhelming desire to watch a lot of TV; I have other things I want to do, like plan things with friends, and for myself—things I've always wanted to do all along. There was even one evening that I came home and took a bubble bath. This may sound trivial, but little things in life are now making me happier. With a glass of wine and bubbles in the tub, I was relaxed. The cat even snuck in and looked at me with his curiosity as to how all those bubbles got there—it was quite amusing. I have all this leisure with no one else in the house and nothing to do. I still wonder how I got to this point. With all of the fights and the tension, now the quiet has calmed me and I hope it gets better and better each day.

Tomorrow, I am going to the company picnic and then to the County Fair with my son and his Grandma—you know, "his" mother. I'm not sure why I'm taking her, but I guess I'm trying to keep the peace in this "love triangle." Well, soon, I won't be able to call her my "mother-in-law" after next month. Just think I have 48 days until I'm single again. It will feel really weird—single again after almost 19 years of commitment to one man who made my life so miserable! It's scary that I put up with those emotions for so very long. I still don't know why I did it.

My girlfriend and I talked about this tonight. I was so miserable. I wanted to leave this earth because of his attitude. My plight started out such a long time ago, but I wanted to stick it out—why? I still don't know. Now, all of those years have passed—was I that hard up that I couldn't find anyone new? Was I that pathetic? Why didn't I realize then what I know now? I must have had blinders on and I was hypnotized into thinking things would eventually work out. My only question is when will she finally realize what I have known for years? She's even got him doing a "honey do" list. He's already refinished her deck, and now her house needs painted, so I'm sure he'll do it, even though he hates doing any construction or household tasks. It's starting…. Will she use and abuse him and then throw him out like the trash? I guess at this point, it doesn't matter—I don't want him back. I don't want a relationship like that ever again! Next time, I will be so picky, I'll probably be considered a "bitch," but, guess what, now I'm in charge!

A good morning has started. I enjoyed myself last night. It was good to see Marie. Even though we talk everyday, it's always good to see her in person. Also, this evening I see my son again, even though it's Friday, we're going to the Fair. I just wonder what my mother-in-law will say to me. She's kept pretty quiet during this whole process. What is she thinking? Is she ashamed of me? Plus, what does she think of her daughter—now they both have something in common—divorce. Her divorce was final over a year ago. It's makes you wonder if divorce runs in their family. I guess I can't talk much; I have several cousins, seven to be exact, that are divorced. But, I never thought it would happen to me, but here I am—in the thick of it! I'm slowly getting used to the idea, but it will take some time to heal. I just want things divided as soon as possible so there's no question—especially about finances We're getting there and I want everything done before "D" day.

Yesterday we had a few words via e-mail, and our son, I guess you could say, started it. He has to be confused, embarrassed, and severely hurt by all of this. He's repeating the lies he thinks he's heard. It's hurtful to me and I let him know that this obviously didn't go over well. I just have to drop it. I don't have the energy to be mad anymore.

Today ended really well. Just before I left for work, a co-worker told me about some new houses for sale that I could probably afford. It was the day of the company barbeque and I was supposed to meet my son and his Grandma after work. I really had to make a quick decision and just go and see them as fast as I could. It was just five minutes away, so I found the location and proceeded to go to the model homes. I went in, told the salesman my situation, and he told me to go view the models that would perhaps fit my needs. One was quite small and didn't have a basement. I also viewed a second home that did have a basement and was a little bigger. I really liked this one; however, I would need at least another $20k to get it. I could use my investment money, but do I want to? How would I tell my ex that I want to move? I guess we could rent out this house I'm currently in, but several things need to be done to it first. There are still so many questions to ponder, and I have to make those decisions by myself. There is no one to make decisions with anymore—how dismal is that? Freedom is one thing, but togetherness is another.

It's Saturday and I have a lot of errands to do today before heading up to the mountains. I may even come back this afternoon and look at that house again that I liked. This morning as I went into town to run my errands, I realized it was the day of the Fair Parade. I didn't have my son today, and then I realized that he would be taking our son to the Parade for the first time—ever. It was always my "job" to do this; but it really wasn't a chore, I enjoyed it. I guess it was when our son turned 5 years old that I started doing this "parade" thing myself, before that we did things together. He hated doing any type of family activity. Well, now that it's his turn to be a parent and since he hates being in crowds, this ought to be interesting. So after a few quick stops in town, I was off to go gambling. The trip is not far from where I live, so it's definitely a day trip. This is something I've always wanted to do, so now I have the opportunity and the means to do it! I even tried to get someone to go with me, but to no avail. So guess what, I'm going anyway, and all by myself! Yes, I said, by myself! Who's the only person you can really rely on when there's no one else around? Yes, yourself! It may be scary, but just do it! I did. I guess I look back on my days when I was single, and I was pretty self-sufficient. So, I don't have any excuses now to not go forth and prosper.

As my journey took me west on the highway, I got closer and closer to the mountains. I passed an area that gets really bad during the winter, and even though it is still summer, I started getting nervous. It wasn't time for snow, but maybe it was a point of no return, but I had to keep going. I never said that my new adventures weren't daunting; it was something I had to push myself to do because I now needed to do this for me. The road trip was only a couple of hours, and I couldn't stop now. I kept going; I wanted to go and I had to make myself do this so I could prove that I can do things on my own. I found a casino parking lot, pulled in, and then entered the front door. It seemed very small and smelled of cigarettes. But, I proceeded up to the window to get a roll of quarters and nickels and then proceeded to the slot machines. At first, it seemed like I was loosing more than I had won, so I went upstairs to play those machines. After putting in just three coins, I realized that I had won 500 nickels. It was just $25, but it was more than I had when I started! After playing a couple more machines, one got tilted by just pushing the "cash out" button. Well, the owner bought me a glass of wine just because the machine was being difficult. My luck was changing. After eating lunch there I went to another casino—there I won $5 by playing just $1. I even played Blackjack for a little while. Wow, I was only there for a few hours, but I really had a good time by myself. Then I realized that I had won around $35—not much, but enough for a tank of gas. Today was fun even though I didn't stay long. It was good to get away and enjoy myself for the first time in a long while. I even got back into town and looked at that house again. Can I really afford to move? I really want to but I'm not sure I can afford it right now. So, perhaps, I'm back at square one; now the decisions and the questions are haunting me once again.

It's Sunday once again. I'm looking forward to church today. I even tried to continue my painting project from late last night to just before I left. I wanted to paint the downstairs bathroom to match the kitchen and family room, but I could only do just a little area until I left. I got to church on time for the singing and then for the service. This minister has got to be reading my mind, once again. For the past three Sundays, he has spoken to my heart in ways that have made me realize that I'm not the only one going through their own personal tragedy. Today's sermon was about how two animals, such as a donkey and an ox, are "yoked" together or attached together somehow—his comparison was with a husband and a wife who are going in different directions and how they are bound to separate in the end. This really hit home—and hard! My ex doesn't want anything to do with the church, or anything to do with what's right and what's wrong. It seems that he's always trying to get away with everything, and he always told me that I was too honest—go figure? Maybe I was too honest, and maybe he wasn't as honest as he should have been. It also seems that this honesty thing is really having issues lately; and I mean all around me. For, this weekend my mom told me that my niece who has only been married three years is now separated. I didn't get the whole scoop, so I had to call my brother who told me that her husband had been messing around and my niece and her one-year old son were living with them. I guess he had been really domineering and degrading to her for a long time. She couldn't even go to work dressed a certain way—he would make her change clothes, and also had to know where she was every minute. Who the hell is this guy? This is not the 16th century, and women don't have to put up with that crap anymore! He's also throwing away his family due to his affair. This world is losing its morality—it's a sorry state of affairs, huh?

I guess my morality has been tested lately too, because my thought process about my ex has made me think evil thoughts about him. Because there have been times in the past few weeks where I have wished for my ex to be dead, or even killed in an airplane crash—once again. Perhaps it's a little drastic, and maybe a little vengeful. However, today when he brought our son back, he told me that when he went to the doctor recently, he had a cancerous spot removed from his forehead. It was a little too close to home. I told him that after September he should get his own health insurance since he wouldn't be on mine anymore. When I suggested that, he acted like he wasn't going to do it because it was too much trouble. I just have a bad feeling about this whole thing. He's really good about blowing off his health. He should go to the doctor more often, but he doesn't. His dad was the same way, and when he got prostate cancer, he had waited too long to get it cured. Then it spread to other parts of his body, and it was too late. He died seven months after we were married.

It's interesting what motivates us to do things and how we do them. As for me, my motivation is to revamp this house. I have taken down several family pictures, and have tried to de-personalize it to the point that this house is no longer my home. Today, I continued that process by finding two more pictures on sale. So far, I've gotten seven pictures for the walls. I'm on a mission, I guess, to redesign "my" home. I want this house to show like a model home. My goal is to get it to the point that when I'm really to sell it, it will show nicely. Maybe I'm trying to distance myself from this place. Perhaps, I'm trying to destroy the bad memories of this house. I mean, the master bedroom use to have a deer head on the wall and a gun cabinet in the corner. It felt like the master bedroom was part of a bachelor pad. It definitely wasn't a single-family dwelling because we weren't a family. Now that I've rearranged the bed, or what's left of it, I am left with a mattress. There's no box springs, no frame, and the headboard is against the wall. The waterbed parts are also against the corner awaiting my efforts to move them into the garage. I'm not sure what to do with this space, but there's one thing for sure, it doesn't look like a bedroom that I want to be in for any length of time. I have three new pictures on the wall, which makes the room a little more neutral and a little more calming. But, it needs to be a retreat, not a hunting trophy room. I've also made it a goal to work on the bathroom cabinets on the second floor. I'm going to sand and paint them too. Even though my son keeps telling me how much I'm ruining the house with my new décor. He doesn't understand; I have to do this for me; it's what I want now. I'm hurting too, and he can only see himself as the one hurting. Maybe it would be better if he were just a baby. Those emotions that a teenager has can never compare to an infant, but I'm sure they're related somehow. I guess I want a romantic and calm feeling after years of ranting and raving from a man that made my blood boil. I can't deal with any more pain in my heart; I want a pleasant surrounding in my life, and after a hard day's work, it's very inviting to have that calm. Call me selfish if you must; but I think I deserve every bit of passion I can get right now. Why not, what did I do that was so bad that he had to have an affair?

Early this morning I woke up thinking about her. What will I do when I finally see her out somewhere? Will she be at the pig roast this Friday? Will her daughter be there too? Part of me is still very angry at her actions. The other part almost feels sorry for her life's work—the part where she wanted to commit adultery to show her girls that is was ok to do this to another woman. What would make a woman and man be so desperate for a different lifestyle and then ruin so many lives along the way? I'm still in awe why this whole situation happened in the first place and why it happened the way it did. There are so many scenarios going through my head on how I will act and what words will come out of my mouth with every new situation. Sometimes I even want to call up my niece's husband and yell at him. I'm not sure how or why I'm even keeping my composure, but maybe it was due to the fact that I think I've known about their actions for so long. Maybe I've wanted it to happen because I was so miserable. A loveless marriage has got to be the worst feeling ever—it was for me. Maybe it was the fact that I would constantly dream about what I would do if he were out of the picture.

I'm not as tired today. It's now Tuesday. I guess Mondays take it out of me—I'm even hungrier on Monday. However, each day seems like it's getting easier to go it alone, but something hits me and I'm almost at Square One again. My anger is subsiding now. It's been 6 ½ weeks since that fateful day. I want so much to forgive them both. Maybe one day in the future I can. Perhaps I just need to see them together in a non-threatening, neutral place. Then reality will hit; I'm sure of it. That pit in my stomach will rumble once again, but maybe that's the bottom I need to hit, so I can get over to the other side.

CHAPTER 10 –

Taking Care of Me

I don't know what it is but every time I try to make a new decision, I can't sleep. Last evening I was looking into life insurance for myself, and the salesman was late getting to my house—that should have been my first clue. I did inquire about a $250k policy and the cost was almost double of what I have now. So, I didn't go with that one; I did however look into an annuity for $50k. The paperwork took forever and I was exhausted. The guy didn't leave until 7:45 p.m. in the evening! Am I making the right decision? I feel as if I'm grasping at straws with every judgment I now have to make. I'm second-guessing myself, and I don't like that feeling. So, after he left, I tried to spend some time with my son to regroup. He was making up a "hangman" game to do at his dad's. I guess I still can't figure out his dad. When he lived here he had too much to do at work, or he had to be somewhere and that location wasn't being at home. Now he's turning into the "perfect" father! He's making time to spend with him on homework, games, and eating dinner together. Is he trying to make up for lying to his family and is he also making amends to his maker? I think he's a little late for both if you ask me. For me every decision I'm now making scares the crap out of me. I have been shaken pretty hard. This sickening feeling makes me wonder if I will ever be happy again or if my life will ever be "normal." It still hits me on certain days and the next year will be interesting. How will each holiday be celebrated and with whom?

The only decision that I have made thus far that really makes me happy is that I am going to a concert on the Western Slope of Colorado. My son also wants to go with me. I have always wanted to see Hewy Lewis and The News, and now I'm finally doing it! I have the tickets and have booked a hotel. It's going to be a couple of hundred dollars, but finally I'm doing something for me.

This whole mess has made me do some soul searching, and with that I am putting myself at the top of the list and doing something for myself, again. So, I treated myself with a new touch phone today. My son was at his dad's for dinner so I got it set up and transferred his account information to my old cell phone since my son had lost his. He thought my phone was really cool, and of course showed me things that I didn't know how to do. I used to do desktop support for a living, now I have a 13 year old telling me how to do things that I didn't understand—go figure! Nonetheless, my time seems so limited lately. I get home and things need to be done, and then it's time to go to bed. I used to watch TV a lot, and now I'm outside more. Besides, doing projects inside, there's no time for TV. My lifestyle has really changed, and I didn't do it on purpose. I now find myself in unfamiliar territory, and I'm not sure if I'm glad about it. For so long I've done things in a certain way and now I feel uneasy and nervous. Will I finally get used to this new way of doing things? Or, will things keep changing for me? When will my life settle down to a suitable norm again? The future is so uncertain right now, and it's Week 7 of my saga—my struggle with life in general continues.

This evening I got take-out for dinner and my son and I had a chance to be together. It seemed like a short meal and after we ate, he went to the office to play on the computer. I decided to finally sit on the sofa and watch TV. Yes, something I really haven't done since "he" left. I just so happened to turn on an episode of Roseanne. It was the same one I had watched a while back where Dan told Roseanne that he had an affair. She was livid, hurt, upset, disappointed—you name it, she felt it. I know her pain; I know what it's like to feel those emotions. Betrayal went through that entire family. Even her son knew something was going on but wasn't given any details. I don't know why I've seen this episode twice now. I hadn't seen it in a long time, and now I've seen it twice in less than two months? What gives?

I guess it's the initial shock of a spouse cheating that makes the "blood" in a family boil from the initiator all the way down to the last child. Divorce or even the initial cause of cheating in a marriage has so many negative effects on the entire family, each person's friends, and their acquaintances. I truly believe if people realized how much hurt, pain, and change this would cause due to their actions, they wouldn't participate in an affair. Or, would they even care? Thank goodness Roseanne had her sister as a part of her support system. My friends have definitely helped me. Some of them know from experience, and some are just there as my crutch. Either way, I'm glad they're there for me. If it wasn't for them, I think I would have lost whatever sanity I still have. Besides, it's not just me going through this mess. This "disease" is all around me. There are ladies at work, one friend just down the street from me, and a few others that are plagued by this disease too that I previously talked about. We all seem to be in the same boat, and we are all leaving our 'port of call' into treacherous waters. Or in other words, our current lives will never be the same ever again—our new lives will be made by our new decisions. But, how will we get there? It's as if our hands need to be held by someone of great importance to us, so we can hold our heads high and keep the strength we know we have within our hearts and in ourselves. Here's a great time to get our strength back and our faith in God. I know it's definitely helping me. As for the men in our lives, I don't think they will ever find the strength they think they have. It's sad, in my experiences, to know that most men have physical strength, but very little have emotional strength. Because, why would they think that another female in their lives will make everything new again? As my ex once said, "same ole cracker." Well, guess what? We all may have the same body parts, but each woman carries within her a different view of how a relationship should work. In my case, some have a more distorted view than others.

Last night was another sleepless night. Maybe it was due to the e-mail I got. I checked my dating service, and there he was—a guy that had e-mailed me about three weeks ago. I thought he was just a disappearing man. You know how those things work— they say they're interested, they get you excited, and then they go away for good. Well, I sent a response back and said that perhaps we could get to know each other better. I guess we'll see how that goes. I want to be excited that I may have another chance for love, but right now I'm having a hard time ever believing those words will ever be in my vocabulary. I guess this will be a waiting game.

Well, tonight is the pig roast. I wonder if "the happy little family" will attend; I guess it doesn't matter—I have to run into them eventually. It's been almost two months and I'm sure my time is running out on that predicament. I'm just so tired. It's been a long week, and I hope I get more energy soon. I can't keep up my pace of worry and despair. Well, I went to the event, and guess what? None of them showed up. I'm not sure if I was disappointed or relieved. The host was "his" friend first, so I wasn't even sure if I was even going to be a part of this event. It did feel strange being there; now that I'm on "his" turf. Since our host was also our investor, he told me that half of our investment was mine, but he had sent it out to him by mistake. I must have had that look on my face, because he then said that my ex couldn't cash the check without my signature. This was good news, but when I tried to reach him, all I got was a voice mail—once again! Was I surprised? Hell no! He never answered his phone unless it benefited himself. I should be used to that response by now, but I'm not. I just want him gone out of everything important in my life. It's always been on his terms—not anyone else's. His time and his projects are more important than anyone else in this world, sad huh? I mean, what would I have to do to get in touch with him if our son was hurt? He only answers his phone when it is convenient for him. In addition, I don't have her phone number either, or does she want it that way? Would she be scared if I had it? I know where she lives—she should be more concerned about that! He had better call me tomorrow. I want one more thing about him out of my life—my money!

The only thing positive today was the guy whom I met through the dating service e-mailed me. He wants to chat via instant messenger, but I'd rather talk via the phone. It has to be hard to get to know someone through words on a computer. What is he waiting for? I gave him my number to call me! Or, is it that guys are slower and non-aggressive in relationships? But, at this point, why do I care? Also, I checked on my e-mail account and the guy that I thought might be a "prospect" is becoming a disappointment. His use of the "English" language is horrible, although his profile was nice. I'm a little concerned—I gave him my phone number to call me, but he'd rather instant message me—what gives? I have heard of scams on this, so I may have just witnessed my first. I guess women are so vulnerable when their hearts are bruised and laying out for every scam artist to touch.

Today, Saturday, was interesting. Since my ex wouldn't call back, I decided to go to his house. Well, my excuse going there will be that our son needed his cell phone charger. I wasn't totally lying, although, it was a good excuse. When we arrived, he was coming out of the garage and he was on his cell phone. I got his attention and then asked him if he had gotten the check and he said, "yes." I then told him that we were headed to the bank

163

and could he meet us there. Well, his immediate priority was his phone call and it would take a while. His response didn't surprise me—his time and his business always took priority over his family, in addition to his lack of faith—you name it! Well, we waited at the bank and after several minutes, I got a call. It was he telling me that he was at the bank and where were we. I guess he didn't realize that when I pointed to the bank where I would be, he didn't pay attention. He went to the branch that he always went to and just assumed we would be there. That was one thing that used to drive me crazy about him—his assumptions were always correct and everyone else was always wrong. I was not, and never was, a priority in his life, nor did he respect me. He even made a comment after we were in the bank depositing the check. I had asked them how long it would take for the bank to verify the funds, and he replied, "Well, is it burning a hole in your pocket?" It was comments like that, which pulled us apart. It seemed as if everything I did or said was wrong in his eyes.

Years of that mouth seemed to break me in different ways. It was also my soul that was hardened, especially when I was around him. Well, I had to brush it off. When we came out of the bank, I asked him for another phone number just in case of emergency. His reply was that his work number and his cell number were the only ones he had, there was no home number—they saved money that way. So, I guess if our son was on his deathbed, his priority would be a business call, and he would call me when he saw fit. Don't get me wrong. I never called him for just anything; I really would have a legitimate reason for calling, but half the time he would say he didn't get the message or he would have some other excuse. Selfishness and greed have once again reared its ugly head. Well, I guess it's just one more thing to add to my anger file.

I couldn't let that situation control the rest of my day because we were going to my Church's picnic. Even though we had several errands to run, we did make it on time. As we sat down to eat, one of the pastors stopped by and said hello. My son happened to leave to get more food, and then he sat down. This man knew I was new at the church and asked how I liked the services so far. I told him that each message seemed to be meant for me. He told me that the Holly Spirit was at work inside me. I wasn't sure what to think at that moment, but I just knew that every time I attended church that the sermon hit me pretty hard. His words were comforting, but at the same time I didn't know what to think. I was glad he stopped to talk—even for just a few minutes. It made me realize that I am not alone in this world—I have people around me who care.

Sunday's sermon was about people who say they're sorry, although they're truly not sorry. When a person really does ask for forgiveness, it's not real if they don't really feel with their emotions.

With this in mind, I don't think my ex ever said he was sorry to me and really meant it. It didn't happen very often, but when it did, there was sarcasm present. It felt like I always had to get his "permission" to buy anything; especially when I went to the grocery store. If it wasn't on my grocery list, I wasn't supposed to buy it. However, sometimes I would just buy it anyway since I forget it write it down. I guess I did it to get back at him for what he did all along—lie. I never said that I was sorry to him because I wasn't. I felt like I was finally exercising my right to do what I wanted—but when I did, there was always hell to pay. Remember the motorcycle he said was a friend's, but he had bought it for himself? Maybe I did this to get back at him, or to just make him mad? Either way, we were at each other's throats for a while. I think that I finally wanted to be in charge of something, and this decision was the beginning of me standing up for myself. All I know is that the next day when I went to work, I left him a letter on the table asking him if this situation warranted a divorce. All day long I contemplated my words in that letter, and was wondering if he did the same. Well, after I got back from work, he seemed remorseful, and as we talked, he said he would go to counseling—well, it was just talk; he never did. That should have been my first clue that our marriage was headed to divorce court.

Maybe church is my therapy. All I know is that every time I go, the tears come from my eyes throughout most of the service. Why do I bother putting on mascara and makeup? It's all gone by the time I leave the building. People, once again, have asked me if I want counseling, but I have declined each time. Am I stubborn? Perhaps. Sometimes, I just want to go it alone—well, almost alone. I'm glad I have so many good friends to be there for me.

This afternoon I even talked to him after dropping off our son. We seem to have good conversations when we do talk—perhaps it's the fact that we talk about our son. That's the only good thing we have in common now. However, I did dig a little deeper today. I asked him about his blood work that he recently had done. He replied that it showed he was a borderline diabetic, and as he put it, if he sneezes, he could have a heart attack. I told him to have a second opinion. Well, he insisted that the results didn't lie and his doctor was one of he best in town. He even stated that his results last year were perfect, and now they were in turmoil. I almost told him, it was all of his "clean living" that made him sick, but I held my tongue once again. That would be my luck—he would die before the divorce is final or shortly thereafter so I would have to still pick up the pieces of my life once again. You know, figure out his insurance policy, get his affairs in order, and get back the things that would go to our son. Then I would have to deal with her. You know, getting back those possessions that are valuable, and then dealing with a funeral. I don't think I have the stomach for any more!

Maybe I'm getting ahead of myself; his dad died of cancer at the age of 57. He's only 46, but 57 years old isn't that far off. These thoughts feel strange to me, but they may happen sooner than I want to guess. Maybe I'm wrong because I could die first. I guess no one plans for death until they're very old. The prime of your life should be just that—Prime!

There was another thing that I got from the sermon yesterday. The Pastor asked the congregation if anyone had ever done something you that you now regret. Well, that's a no-brainer!! This brings me back to my decision to confront him. I guess my decision continued what my ex started, and then the snowball effect began. It's almost like a trickle of water coming from a dam, and with one quick decision, I got a sledgehammer and made that small crack into a large hole that became a gusher. Was I wrong to want to know the truth? I don't think so! I was obligated to myself to get to the truth so I could finally forgive him and then move on with my life. Yes, I said forgive him. I've struggled with that emotion for several weeks now, but I think I'm getting closer to that point when I can say it out loud.

It's Tuesday; one more night of sleep interrupted by thoughts of insecurity. At 4:30 a.m. it was like a light bulb went off in my head. I woke up thinking about the investment check—did it clear yet? Would there be a problem with the funds? Well, I had to check my on-line bank account to ease my mind. My account reveled what I needed to know—it had cleared, and now I had a deposit in my account that I've never seen before. You would think that I could get back to sleep, but no, it was not to be. Now I had a new dilemma—how do I invest it? I've got an idea, but can I be certain of the outcome? After what I've been through, I'm not sure of anything anymore. I even sent out e-mails asking for advice on investments. One person wanted me to invest in a life insurance/annuity account. When his follow-through didn't happen, I cancelled my contract. The other guy wanted me to invest and he bragged about how much money he usually charges for his services as a financial planner. There I go, getting around another man who thinks he knows it all! Well, guess what? I'm not dealing with someone like that—I just got rid of an arrogant asshole in my life; I'm not getting another this soon; maybe never! I'm just not into men telling me what to do right now. Maybe, I'll never be; who knows? Right now I'm doing what I want and buying what I want. I've been so suppressed for so long, I guess I'm finally acting out my emotions. What do I have to lose? I'm starting over and I have the money to do it—within reason, of course.

Trying to keep my composure is easier said than done, but I have to do this. I guess experimentation is natural while going through a divorce. It's just the way you do it that matters. It seems everyone has advice for you, but it's ultimately your decision what you do to keep your sanity. Keeping sensible about things is easier said than done, though. Emotions are so up and down and they seem to run your life way too easily for a very long time. I hope I pass this test soon—It's too hard. I don't even know how to study for something like this.

Today, more changes are happening in my life. The sales lady, that I spoke to on Saturday, called to tell me the bedroom set I wanted is now available. I went looking for new furniture then, but couldn't find what I wanted, but now it was going to be mine. After work, I went to the store and paid cash for it. I haven't paid cash for anything that costly before in my life. It was inspiring and motivating since I could now make decisions without "him," because now I could get what I wanted. It's so empowering to make your own decisions, but also scary to second-guess yourself. It's also frightening that you don't have a "back up" person or plan in your life to lean on for anything. This new experience allowed me to "not" ask permission to do something for once in almost two decades. There was a time before my son was born when I did this, but it was so long ago, I think I forgot what it was like to have that independence.

Little do I know it, but my life is changing for the good. However, Mary is once again struggling. Her significant other has such a hold on her. She still lacks the self-confidence she so desperately needs to be self-sufficient. I just wish I knew what to do for her. Her income is limited, and with few assets she feels that she's trapped in a life that will never change. His emotional hold on her makes the littlest things in her life become thresholds to the next activity. She cries at the drop of a hat and that can't be good for anyone. I know she's got counseling at least once so far, but years of emotional control have made her a poignant wreck. My other co-worker, Leslie, however has love blooming all around her. She is going on a trip in October and she's never looked so happy. It's really strange to see all three of us at different stages of a divorce. The beginning can be very hurtful with emotions of despair, hopelessness, and not knowing where to turn next. Even not knowing how to begin the process of splitting up can be an event in itself. The paperwork alone can drive you crazy. But, as each day passes, the emotions seem to settle; although all of our emotions can run at their peak sometimes. I hope Mary will get to that point. It's mid-August, and her dilemma started in late June and she's still a wreck even though her dilemma happened one week after my blow up. My life is starting to settle down now. Two months—just think—60 days of life changing events, but I'm surviving.

It's Thursday; the day he and his new chick go out of town for his business trip. I'm not sure how I feel about that. I guess life goes on without him since I am not in the picture—for the most part. If it were me with a new life, would he be jealous? Or, would he realize that I could survive without him? So, with that in mind, he obviously thinks he can survive without me—this is really different for me. I hope I can survive. This whole mess is now out in the open, so why should I care? My son comes back early to stay with me, not on Sunday like the norm, but today. I think I'm more concerned about him than my ex; I have to admit. I've wished, once again, that his plane would crash, but what would that prove? I may have these thoughts every time he travels, but hopefully, I'll get over them soon. If this would happen, the logistics of the whole thing would be a mess. Where would he be buried, if his body were found? What would happen to her daughters and her home and possessions? A new catastrophe, or you can call it Part II of the adultery saga would now begin. My emotional roller coaster would begin all over, so hopefully I'm not sending out bad vibes to the spirit world to take over!

I'm in uncharted territory now, and so is Mary. She hasn't filed for divorce yet; I guess she's waiting for him to start that process. Maybe they're just at odds with each other; who knows? Her ex is playing a lot of mind games with her and it's really affecting her emotional state. I don't understand why he is acting like that. Does he feel he has to be in charge or in control and does he feel his actions are compensation for his untimely demise? Is he struggling to find himself and he knows that he can manipulate her so he can finally get what he wants out of life? Why does his lack of strength in this situation that he created for himself, have to now be her problem?

I guess the only way to look at divorce is to see the humor in other situations. For example, last night I was painting my son's room and then putting some things away, and then my cat decided to get curious, and just happened to go into the linen closet, of which I closed the door and didn't realize he was there. It was at least two hours later when I finally found him. It was kind of funny because he was so happy to see me, and just couldn't get enough of me petting him. I guess life continues even though the world crumbles around you.

This evening my son came back to my home early, for the week, since his dad went to Utah on a business trip, and she went with him. It didn't bother me until my son told me that he made it there ok. So, why did it bother me now? Was it the fact that he always thought I didn't travel well? He constantly told me that I took too many clothes, and that I didn't pack as good as him. Maybe that was why we hadn't gone on vacation together for the last three years. Besides, it always seemed like my way of traveling was always wrong.

Plus, there's still a part of me that wants to get back at him, and since he didn't want most of the furniture except his dresser; the decisions are now mine. I have a right to dispose of it, right? Well, I think so. Besides I bought a new table and chairs—all by myself—without his permission and with my money!

I think being empowered during and after a divorce has got to be the greatest cure for this hangover! This same feeling was the same one I had when I was single, and now is my chance to get it back. Although my son thinks I am destroying the house by changing it with new furniture and paint. He cannot realize that I am now gaining my independence again. I hope someday he will understand my reasons that I have for my life right now; his resistance to my change is getting quite old. I know he hasn't liked "change" since he was 18 months old, but I'm trying to coax him over to my side now. Nonetheless, I'm having an intense time accomplishing this task. I am in the process of talking to him about how his dad changed my life in a very dramatic way and how I now need my independence acknowledged. But, how do you do that with a 13 year old? This struggle is making me rack my brain for answers along with the other answers I so desperately need.

I just wish Mary could gain her independence. I hope therapy gets her where she needs to be emotionally and financially. She feels very depressed since "his" lead brick hit her so hard. I knew mine was coming; she didn't even have a clue her ex was committing "stupid." I know she's having a hard time relating to me. However, I feel that I'm a lot stronger than her since I was on my own several years before I was married. I had time to gain my independence; she was 17 when she married her ex—not enough time to gain the strength needed to be on your own.

I feel she doesn't want to say a lot to me since I'm handling my situation in a different manner than her. I know she wants to be at a stage where she is moving forward. I just wish she was at the same point as me—you know—ready to kick him to the curb, both emotionally and physically and never look back. I guess the commitment you have to make to yourself to go on, has to be a 24/7 one. Each day will throw you challenges, but you must take each minute, hour, and day for what it's worth and get through the situation as best as you can even though your heart is breaking. I guess my best example of getting through a situation happened last night when my son got really mad at me for buying new furniture. He said that he was going to tell his dad what I did. I tried to explain to him that his dad is now living in a nice house with nice things and I wanted nice things too. So, he started to make a list of things that I was going to replace. For a long time, he's had a habit of writing things down that he needs to ponder on later. From songs on the Internet to various songs that he likes to listen to on the radio, and now to what I'm doing, so his dad can stop me. I am sad that he can't move on like I have, and I have contemplated on this for several weeks now. I even woke up around 2 a.m. this morning, and I think I've finally figured out why he's so upset. Since his dad and I split, his world has also been split. His dad got rid of me, so he's probably thinking that I'm in the process of getting rid of everything in my

175

life too—to include him. He's struggling to hold onto whatever is familiar in his life. His insanity is showing and I didn't get it until now. I have to explain this to him in a different way—especially, before my new furniture comes tomorrow. He has to know that I would never "throw" him away as I would a piece of furniture.

Speaking of furniture, I had a guy from work who wanted my kitchen table. I've given him my address, my cell number, and when I was available. He's had three days to let me know if he wanted to see the table and chairs. I even had to e-mail him late yesterday to see if he was still interested. Since I'm doing more work to sell this to a "man" than I wanted to, I have another person interested. My neighbor's daughter wants to see it. Maybe I'm getting hard nosed or my sense of self is getting stronger, or is it that I'm not putting up with any more bull shit from people—men in general. It feels strange, maybe a little weird to have this new found strength. Maybe I've always had it, but for the past 19 years, I've put it away in a box and shoved it to the back of the closet for safe keeping. I think we all have inner strength, but something has happened to us to make us forget where we've put it, or our significant other has taken it from us without our permission or even our realization. I believe it's our God-given right to succeed in life—with or without another person's permission.

My strength seems to be growing, but my son is not going along for the ride. He is so upset that the old furniture is going away.

I spoke to him several times and told him I wanted something new—perhaps a new beginning for me. The more I told him this, the angrier he got. I finally told him that the old furniture held so many bad memories for me, so I wanted to start fresh with new memories. I hope this works. I'm getting very burnt out trying to explain or even justify my actions to a teenager. I just wish I could get him into a counseling program that I enrolled him in, but he is still on a waiting list from the call I got last night. This program said that the waiting list is very long and they don't foresee him getting in any time soon. In the meantime, I'm trying to answer his questions and guide his actions and responses to each thing that happens. Each day is a challenge and I'm taking each challenge one bite at a time.

Today, Sunday, began as usual. My son was reviewing the newspaper and then we got ready for church. The only different thing was that my ex wanted our son after services this morning. After church was over, we went out to my vehicle and then I called him to let him know that we could come over. He was at his office in town and preceded to tell me that his truck wasn't in the front of his office; it was in the shop. Ok, I though, maybe he got a ride there. Well, when we arrived, there he was with her vehicle parked right in front. Should I have been surprised? I guess not. He also told me that he wanted our son until Wednesday. This kind of threw me. He didn't run this change by me first. I wanted to ring his neck at this point and the moment became a little tense. We were almost at each other's throats and I realized my son was just feet from both of us, so I cooled my jets, once again. In addition, we got into a heated conversation since we both planned to take our son to different events in September. Go figure? They were both on the same dates and now my ex wanted me to change my plans even though I had already spent money for the both of us. He got mad at my plans and said that since I had our son that week, that he guessed he didn't have a say in which activity he should attend. I guess he was trying to make me look bad although he was the one who started the fight. Well, he's going with me—my son's been preparing himself to take a trip with his mom. It's almost like he's trying to intimidate or control me once more. Well, guess what, sorry dude—not this time! My destiny is in my hands now and he will not change me anymore. It's almost like when couples get married, the woman seems to be the one who is expected to mold to her new husband—well, at least it was like that back in the 50s. In our relationship, it was he who held the whip and chair, and tried to keep me in a cage for almost two decades. What happened to "give and take?" How did I choose someone so controlling and deceitful? His ways are ones that I could not predict, nor could I control. He had a habit of getting furious one minute, and then the next minute it was as if he had forgotten what went on during the entire heated conversation. As for me, I would dwell on that stuff for hours and sometimes days. I'm getting better, though, I'm starting to brush off his comments sooner than later so that I can free myself of this disease called divorce.

In addition to it being Sunday, church this morning was another addition to my situation. The Pastor mentioned how finances and their success or failure is related to giving. My ex was always trying to make a buck on some new venture he constantly tried. But, he never gave to anyone financially or otherwise, especially to the church. He never gave to charities, his friends, and anyone else in need. The only place he was giving was to his retirement fund—or lack thereof. This was another way we differed. I constantly gave to charitable organizations, people at work, and to people at Christmas. I didn't mind, on the contrary, I really enjoyed giving to people. It made my heart full when I knew someone else could get use and even joy out of what I provided. How could he not feel the same? A cheerful giver is a matter of the heart. Was his heart so black that it couldn't pump blood to his vital organs? Or did he even have vital organs? I can't imagine how cruel and heartless someone can become that his or her life is that sorrowful. I mean, all of his life he struggled with that negative word, "try." As he would put it, "trying is failure." But, doesn't a person have to try in order to succeed?

Another work week has begun—it's now Monday again. The weekends seem to fly by and I'm at work all the time now. Well, right before work I called the publishing company and left a message. I want to become an author, and I'm going for it! It's scary, but I've wanted this accomplishment in my life for a very long time. There's an old saying, "if you want something you've never had before, you have to do something you've never done before to get it." I'm taking a lot of chances lately, and it feels good until I sit down and think about my actions. I'm totally out of my comfort zone, but I must do this for me. I guess in order to skydive; you have to take the first step out of the airplane, right? Will I fail? Who knows, but I'm going to do things now that must be done; I cannot contemplate failure now. I can't make excuses anymore about anything. I can't be stagnant and see him getting on with his life and succeeding, and me not moving forward. The way I see it, he now has a "sugar momma," who provides him with a nice house to live in and a SUV to drive. Her SUV is a nice vehicle and he's proud of how it makes him feel when he drives it; I guess she makes him feel good too, but I can't dwell on that issue. Also, when he talks about his "piece of crap" truck, he gets frustrated—I felt the same when a car I had years ago kept breaking down. I would drive this car, I would never know when it would leave me sitting next, and although, I had our son with me many times, he didn't care that we could be in danger. That's past history now, but

I sometimes dwell on the fact that he didn't care about us the way he now seems to care about her and their living arrangement. It makes me wonder if she'll dump him because he's such a liability? If not, and they get married some day, well, guess what? Now he's her problem and not mine! Will justice finally be served to me on a silver platter? Perhaps, and then maybe I won't care by then.

As I ponder other women who've been dumped, I sometimes think of my little sister from the Big Sister Program. Her dad once lived with her and her "then" husband. Her dad's illness must have been the last straw in their relationship. For, one evening, her husband came home early from work and surprised her when she opened the door. He was just sitting there on the couch, in the dark, and said and he had been unhappy for a very long time and wanted a divorce. Within an hour he had three of his buddies, all with pickup trucks, there at their house to load up his possessions so he could move out. She was dumbfounded and left shaken. In addition to springing this on her, he emptied the checking account and left her with nothing. She was so traumatized that life was extremely difficult for the next two years. In order to support herself and her sickly dad, she worked two jobs and just dealt with life as it came. After this two-year time frame, her dad died from his illness and then she was left completely alone. I guess her only saving grace was her strength that she says I helped instill in her.

As a Big Sister, I worked feverishly to get her out of her shyness when she was just 14 years old and to help her grow emotionally. It must have worked, because people now do not believe that she was ever shy. She does not put up with anyone's crap and stands up for herself. I am so glad I was there to direct her in a positive light. Now, years later, she is happily married once again and is now expecting her first child. I am so proud of her for what she has accomplished in her life and her story has enlightened me to continue my journey even though the struggles I have to face are very similar to hers. I guess the best revenge couldn't even be called revenge in her case. She's seen her ex in several places, in addition to her friends seeing him, and each time he was dating a younger woman—at least half his age. His once debonair demeanor has now been replaced by less than appropriate grooming habits, and a profound loss of hair upon his head. When I knew him, he was quite handsome, but I guess not anymore. He's let himself go—a lot! My little sister is quite proud of herself. With every bit of trauma in her life, she kept her credit good by having those two jobs, made it financially, and found the love of her life! Good for her!! There is life after divorce, but no one can convince you of that fact when that word is thrust upon you so hard. Day to day events are just one of life's little lessons that we don't want to listen to, but we are made to listen by powerful forces around us.

As for me, I have proceeded forward with my next goal, I met with the lady to purchase life insurance for myself. I didn't realize that when I originally got life insurance, it was 16 years ago, and it was for a term of 15 years at the same price. It had expired last year and now the initial premium was going up again. I guess I didn't get the details back then on the process—another thing I let my ex handle. I let him make most of the decisions in my life and I didn't realize it—why didn't I pay more attention? Why wasn't I more involved in the big decisions? Maybe, I felt there was a secure force field around me with him in my life and I was comfortable. It's amazing to look back now and realize how much of a crutch he was in my life, and how I allowed it to happen.

Today is another life-altering decision that I have to make. The cable bill is in his name and I have to get him off the statement—just one more thing to irritate me. It's kind of like when you get married and the woman "has" to change her name. Well, I guess she really wouldn't have to, but it seems like it happens that way a lot. Just think, your social security card, credit cards, driver's license, bank accounts, etc., all have to be changed—or do they? Why do women put up with this stuff? We are inconvenienced to the hilt, and men don't do a damn thing! Well, getting everything into my name, I guess, is one more victory for me, or one more liberating event to my acclaim. I guess I'm glad we're still on talking terms—at least for now.

My other goal is to still work on the house. I painted some more last night in the laundry room. The tan-colored paint has now erased the dark green color that was once there. It's lighter now, and it's as if a light bulb came on and it has now been refreshed. Maybe that's why I'm so into painting certain rooms. I guess I needed to feel renewed—you know, that feeling you get after a summer rainstorm that clears the air with a new smell? All the bad air has been replenished with a freshness that makes you feel good. I guess I lost that feeling a long time ago, and now it's my turn to feel good about myself once again. So, now the world is at my fingertips—all I have to do now is touch, feel, and grab on for the ride of my life.

I think I'm on the downhill slide today. I got the last bill put into my name, and my life and auto insurance policies are both in the works. I just have to review the paperwork to see if it Is accurate, sign it, and then write a check. Lately, it seems like everyone wants money from me. Yea, sure, the furniture cost quite a bit, but I'm also changing every other thing in my life too. The months of August and September seem to have lots of bills any way, but this year it's coming to me in droves. Between changing everything into my name, and then dealing with everything else that comes along, it's very tiring. It's definitely a roller coaster ride, and I don't want to be in the front seat of this ride for very much longer.

When the divorce is final, I'll also have to change my will—which is currently in a draft form for now. I'm going to get that notarized and a copy sent to my brother. In addition, I'll have to get my retirement account changed too. Will it ever end? God, I hope so. I'm so mentally drained right now that I'm ready to explode! I'm just glad it's amicable thus far. I've heard of divorces that won't ever end since an "ex" is staying in the picture and trying to drag their significant other down to the bottom of the well with them. I know I've said it before, but the strength I've gotten from my friends and my church has helped more than I can ever say.

I'm beginning to feel like a broken record because last night was another sleepless one. My cat started it by waking me up at 3 a.m. I don't know why he needs my love and attention at that hour, but he does apparently. So, of course, my mind had to start racing once again. What about my bills? What is my upcoming trip going to cost me? Am I going to make it financially by myself? I kept trying to convince myself that I couldn't do anything about these questions this early in the morning, and even later on today or tomorrow, but it was harder to convince myself than I thought. So, of course, when the alarm went off at 5:15 a.m., I literally fell out of bed, from the sudden noise. I think I even portrayed my best zombie impression for the rest of the day with my lack of sleep.

In addition to not being able to sleep, my middle ear seems to be clogged, so I can't hear as well as I should. I had hoped it would be better today, but after the doctor told me that it's wasn't infected, I was relieved. I guess my tolerance for everything has been tested this year. Needless to say, I'm not making any progress to stop the bleeding. This year started with my son getting into trouble at school and then I hired a school advocate to have a meeting. Next, it was a medical issue with my son, and now I'm on the downhill slide on my way to "divorce central." No wonder I'm tired and confused with life in general. I even have 15 days of vacation saved up at work, which means that I haven't been on a real vacation in a long time, and I don't know what it feels like to relax. The last time I had a week of vacation was almost 3 ½ years ago. Yes, I've had a day off here and there, but not a full week at once since then.

My life used to be more settled, more of a routine. I can't even get myself ready in the same time frame any more. I need more time for everything, and why? Is not a minute still 60 seconds? I've even prided myself in getting things done in a timely fashion, but lately my personal life is lacking in that area. However, I'm ok at work, for now at least. I can keep my concentration there— thank God for that. I'm at work everyday, but I'm very tired. My ear is bothering me and I am having a hard time keeping awake. My heart hurts so much, and I'll probably never get the questions answered for which I need a conclusion. What was his reasoning for hurting me to the point of a breakdown? I mean I never totally lost it, but this sadness is quite overwhelming and it has stifled my self worth. Besides, how will I now give my total heart to someone new without wondering if it will happen again? This pain is so fresh that it may never go away. However, I can't dwell on emotional issues right now since I've got to finalize my auto insurance policy today. I keep getting off track, and I have to constantly regroup with everything. Nonetheless, I did accomplish something major today—I paid off some other furniture that I bought recently. At least there's one thing completed in my life. If I can just get more things settled, then I'd feel much better and on solid ground, or at least the ground would stop shaking. Right now, the earthquake is having after shocks, and I'm caught near the fault line, which doesn't allow me to get away too quickly.

This whole process is making me feel like I'm losing my mind. I still can't keep track of the flood of changes and the new things hitting me from all sides. I'm a pretty good organizer, but these last few days have made me rethink how I do things. Today is the 27th of August, and it just happens to be 27 more days of marital misery, and then I'll be free. But, what does "free" really mean? Free of someone telling me what to do and what not to do? Will I be free to come and go as I please—within reason, of course due to home and work obligations? I just want to know when my new "norm" will kick in. Or, will anything ever be considered normal again? I never thought that I would be a member of this new club, but now that I'm here, I have to learn the rules. I have no choice—not anymore—I'm a permanent member of the "D" club.

This evening my schedule was yet again interrupted. He wanted our son in martial arts, so he was under the impression that our son and ten other classmates would be walking three blocks to the Dojo. Well, it was more than three blocks, and only one other classmate would attend, but only after his mom dropped him off there. So, I had to pick him up from school and drop him off, run home to prepare dinner, and then run a quick errand before I picked him up once again. At 6:30 p.m. when I picked him up, he greeted me and then complained of a migraine. He said that he didn't want to go back. I didn't know what do. His dad wants him to continue in this activity; I'm torn. It's three days a week, and getting him to and from there is quite the chore. Am I getting lazy? Do I like my newly found freedom too much now? I'm feeling slightly guilty, but I haven't had much freedom in the past 13 years of parenthood. I've been the parent, who's done almost 99 percent of everything for our child since he's been alive, and now I have a chance to relax a little; I'm beginning to like it. I can just see it now; this will get in his way too, and he will ask his new chick to play "mom." I know him far too well, if he gets too busy, or needs to do something for himself, he'll pawn off our son to someone else until it's convenient for him to have our son back. He's done it before. No wonder I want some freedom. Don't get me wrong I love my son. I just want the same "time off" as he's had for the past 13 years. So, what is this new found "dad license" he's acquired? He always said that if he were in charge, things would flow more smoothly. Well he's in charge when our son is there—let's see how he likes being a "full time" dad for once in his life. Besides, he's always been a creature of habit; we'll see how long it takes for her to get sick of his irritating ways.

This whole process has made me feel like a teenager again, and I don't mean in a good way. It's almost like going through puberty again, but it has nothing on a divorce situation. The emotional ups and downs are 100 times worse, and now you're more responsible, or at least you're supposed to be more responsible. Maybe I need a vacation; my body and soul are tired both emotionally and physically. I am drained. But, how do I fix me? I am so strong, or at least I think I am, but I can fall apart so easily, and right now I am as fragile as glass. One wrong move and I can flip off and on like a light switch. One good example was when I got really angry today. I couldn't get the cable guy to call me on my cell or home number, or did he? No, he didn't! He left a smart-ass remark on my home number that he guessed that I wasn't home, so I needed to reschedule my appointment for another time! If he had paid attention to my instructions on which phone number to call me, then I would have my Internet fixed today. This event was my downhill slide for the rest of the day. Every little thing after that really angered me. I'm really easy going, but that really ticked me off for a long time. How can someone be furious one minute, and then happy the next? I feel like I'm back in school and I'm failing my finals even though I studied really hard? Calgon, take me away!

CHAPTER II – ⋆

Sliding Backwards

*L*ast night I had another conversation with my son. He's still confused about what his dad did to our family. It was a difficult decision, but I talked to him about the subject of adultery, what wedding vows mean, and the Ten Commandments. I basically told him that what his dad did was wrong and used those subjects as examples for my defense. His face said it all. I really think he got it, because he kept telling me that he was "watching" them and every time they kissed, he was taking notes. I told him that it didn't matter any more. It's all out in the open, and it will not prove anything. That part of our conversation didn't go very far. He's determined he can change the situation between the three of us, but he can't. It's just like me at the age of 8; I was determined to change my dad's drinking problem. He was an alcoholic, and I just knew I could make him stop and that I could also implement prohibition once again. My high hopes did not come true, but no one could convince me otherwise. In a way, my son is just like me—determined and stubborn and ready to swing with the world by its tail and save its passengers. Little do we know, especially when we are young, the world revolves around us without our permission?

Today, I had another chore to do. I went to get a new charger for my Blue tooth since it's disappeared. I couldn't buy a replacement one, so I had to buy a brand new unit. If I were still with him, I would have had to ask permission. You know that "Mother May I" game you played when you were a kid where every question was a permission slip waiting to happen? Well, I'm responsible for my own decisions and my own money now. Don't get me wrong; I'm not overspending. I'm just buying what I've wanted for very long time and couldn't have because of him, but I'm keeping track of my budget. Do I miss having someone tell me what to do? Well, that's a big NO!

It's been 10 weeks tomorrow that his secret was let out of the bag. I'm really starting to feel more comfortable once again. But that could change really quickly if something happens to bring back these memories. I guess every situation is different, and the divorces going on around me at work are all different. Leslie continues to have a great time since her divorce. Her new love interest wants her and her son to meet his step mom—she's a nervous wreck. Even though she's really in to this guy, she's also determined to never get married again until her son is out of the house, nor even live with him. Maybe certain priorities are at the top of her list, but she does seem really happy. I hope to get there someday. The only good thing happening to me is that I now fit into a pair of jeans that are one size smaller than before. I guess it's the little things in life that I must now focus on to start me back on that happy trail. If only my son could join me on this path.

I guess my talk with my son last night was memorable, because today when my son went with his dad for the day, he spoke out at her, and I heard about it later. What part of this "situation" went wrong for him? I guess respect in relationships and the influx of adultery was too much for him. After explaining what wedding vows should mean between two people, and what happens when one person strays, the emotional flood gates open up and everyone within 50 feet is affected. He was so angry at what all this meant, that he told her that she was the one who caused his parents to divorce. Her expression was, "What?" Then, he immediately changed the subject to something else, so I guess our talk really hit home. I guess he scored "two points" now! I just don't know what got in him to say those words to tell her off, but I was really proud of him for sticking up for his mom. I also wondered what she now thinks of her actions, and how she really feels about this whole mess. Is she finally feeling guilty? Has she finally realized what she tore apart? Probably not—she's just like him; she gets what she wants and no one will stand in her way; even me. I also was curious if his dad had heard the conversation; my son said that he didn't. However, I'm sure he had an earful from her after he dropped off our son with me.

The conversation even got a little strange when he dropped off our son at my house. My ex acted like he wanted to talk. But, he really had nothing to say—he was babbling as usual. Finally, after the air got a little "cold," he said he had to go and then drove away. Maybe I was reading more into it, but it almost seemed like he missed "us." That was a little too weird. If anyone thinks I want his ass back in my bed, they must be crazy! I wouldn't trust him again as far as I could throw him and at this point, it's about two inches. My life is starting over, and it will be without him! My son still seems to think that if his dad came back home, all would be forgiven, and we could be a happy family again. I tried to enforce, with my son, about my childhood with my dad. I've tried over and over again to tell him that my dad was an alcoholic and when I was younger than him, I was going to change my situation too. I was on a mission and I was bound and determined to make it happen--just like him. For years, it seemed as if I could accomplish this task. It never came to fruition and I tried to explain this to him and tell him one's actions to make something a certain way, will not always make it so. Of course, he didn't get anything out of this one-way conversation. Did I expect him to understand? No, not really, because I never got it either when an adult tried explaining it to me. He has a lot of what I had in me at his age. You know—the power to change the world around you—but not the skills. It's a great effort, but no less a futile one. It's one in which the effort needs to be let go.

It's my week again. He has plans to go hunting; his yearly trip. He's planned this every year since I've known him. When we first met and he first learned of my birthday, he first informed me that this day was the start of dove season. So, I guess I was thoroughly forewarned from the beginning. I really didn't mind, but I did want dinner and a present out of it since he wasn't here for the big day. This year, I guess, the topic of discussion with his hunting buddy will be our "so-called" marriage. This same "buddy" was the best man at our wedding. I wonder how my ex has explained his actions to him along with his friends and acquaintances? Do they feel sorry for me? Am I to blame because I was at fault in their eyes? There are still so many questions that still go through my mind. The only good thing is that I don't dwell on them as much any more. I'm still scared, but I have to move those feelings to the other side of my life so they don't totally engulf me.

My thoughts go back to yesterday when my son blamed her for the divorce. Did she finally get it? You know, that word—adultery? Do her girls know the whole story—my bet is, No! I even wonder what my soon-to-be ex mother-in-law thinks and if she still wants to hang out with me anymore. I even called her today to see if she wanted to go out on Tuesday—you know, my birthday. Now it was my turn to finally get my chance at a guilt trip on her, the way she does everyone else. I told her that I hadn't heard from her and since I won't be her daughter-in-law soon, I figured she had forgotten about me. She was a little dumbfounded, but recovered quickly with a remark like she didn't realize it was 24 days away from those papers that would change my life. Gee, she may even have another daughter-in-law soon. Now, someone else will have the opportunity I've had for almost two decades to deal with her and her attitude.

I know I keep bringing up church, but as the week wore on, Sunday was here again. Plus, every service seems to just hit home more and more. Today, the message was about relationships and how a loving and giving one is vital for one to thrive. You must show how much you care by giving and sharing, and by putting the interests of others above your own. Being a person of your word is another vital ingredient. We didn't have that in our marriage. He always put his interests above his family. His health, his job, and his outside interests were always more important than anyone other than himself. I felt like I took a back seat to him in so many ways. He even traveled to foreign countries and several U.S. states, and I was never invited to go with him. I don't think I'll ever know why he acted in this way, but does it really matter now?

I guess his interests were his own, and every day of my new life had its own issues that reared their ugly head. For example, last night was a little unnerving for me. Around 1 a.m. I heard my son having a bad dream. He called out for his dad several times in a very scared, concerned voice. It woke me up from a dead sleep. As I lay there, I listened to see if he got up, but he never did. I, finally got up to see if he was still asleep, and he was. What was he dreaming about, and will he remember this dream in the morning? He's done this before, but not since my ex moved out. This divorce has really been hard on him. Every emotion you can think of, well, he's experienced it. I'm just glad it hasn't been a divorce where the emotions are high between his dad and me. I guess I need to count my blessings and pick my current and future battles with the both of them.

Today is Monday and the last day of August—just one day from my birthday. There's just 23 more days from my freedom. This evening, I picked up my son from his Grandma's house. There was a present on the table, of which my son told me was mine. Some how I guess I will graciously accept it tomorrow.

This year is so different. The whole atmosphere at her house has turned cold. I feel like a stranger in her home now. She's also been really short in our conversations—more than normal.

Even though my son is included in "their" family—I am now considered the outsider. I have been pushed aside like yesterday's paper. I don't belong in this family any more and that gut wrenching feeling has come back with a vengeance. Maybe it never left, so when will this sickness finally leave me? Will I ever have a part of a family unit again? My family lives over 1,500 miles away. All I have here is my son and my friends now. It's almost like it was when I first moved here almost 21 years ago. My little sister lived with me at that time, and it was just the two of us. I had my friends at work, but that was it. I didn't have a "wife-in-law" like I do now. Which is worse? Having an "ex-family," or none at all? This loneliness still haunts me, and even though I'm a strong person, I want to cry, I want to scream, and I want to tell the world what a bastard he was to me for so many years. I want to pull her hair out and totally embarrass her in front of her peers. I don't like feeling this way, because now I'm the outsider and everyone's life seems so much more perfect than my own. However, I can't think that way now; I have to be strong if only for my son. He can't see me weak, or should he? Should he see me cry and show the same emotions that he is feeling? At this point, things are still fuzzy. Just when I think I have a handle on life, someone changes the placement of the handles. Can I make it until "D" day—time will only tell?

My son even made a comment that set me off today. He said, "I think she's pregnant!" When he said that I didn't know what to say. Wouldn't that just be the icing on the cake? It would certainly explain a lot, but how in the world will this all play out? I hope he's wrong, but I did ask him to ask her. I think it's time for her to pay the piper. She's been too "innocent" in this whole mess and I want her to suffer as much as I have. How dare her act as if she deserves a new life after she tore mine apart! Life needs to get more complicated for their relationship. Just as they both destroyed my life, I think its time for them to come to a reality summit just like I have.

It's Tuesday, my birthday, and the day started out really early this morning. I awoke at 3:26 a.m. from a very vivid dream. My ex, our son, and I were in our home, and as I looked out the window, the floodwaters were fast approaching us. My son, in the dream, was only a toddler. As I tried to pack some clothes for him so we could make our escape, I was very meticulous and took careful note to fold them just right. Now, the floodwaters were getting closer, and the house was surrounded. Just then the house was knocked off its foundation and we were free floating. We hung on for dear life and watched out the window as the 100-year flood carried us down the river. I hung on tight to my son, but my ex was nowhere near the two of us, and he never clung to me during this entire event. It was so real that I awoke suddenly, and then I couldn't get back to sleep. So, for the next two hours I lay there in bed too afraid to go back to sleep. I don't think I wanted to find out the ending, but would I even go back to sleep and continue it anyway? This dream was an omen, and I know what it was trying to tell me. The adventure we were all on wasn't going to end anytime soon, and my son was very vulnerable to everything that was still to happen. My ex wasn't the total cause of everything, but a powerful force had entered our lives and was going to change it forever. The dream did not have an ending; maybe I had to wake up so that I could write my own ending? All I know is that I woke up from fear. I think my brain is on overload, because there's too much information circulating in that gray matter up there at the present time. I guess all of the information that I don't want to deal with seems to come out when I sleep. Why does divorce cause so much grief? Maybe it's an ending to what once was a beginning of a life moment. Being strong through this kind of crisis isn't all it's cracked up to be. A better description would be a death that never seems to die; or, at least something that needs to go to bed for an eternity. God help me; especially through this, of all days, my birthday.

I talked to a friend today, and we discussed how relationships change when you get divorced. Wel the friends of my soon-to-be-ex are now in a position where they have to choose their loyalty to one or the other of us. In my case, I haven't heard from his friends. His sister won't even call me. I didn't really talk to her much in the last few months anyway. We really didn't have much in common and our value systems are quite different. This divorce has hit me hard. It seems as if someone left the door to the frig open and the cold has escaped somehow, and all of the air is coming my way. The cold shoulder treatment has just begun I guess. Is their loyalty going to his side, or do they feel guilty if they would even talk to me again? I didn't start this affair thing! He cheated—not me! Why should I be punished because he has wandering body parts? Maybe I'll never have an answer, but does it really matter now? I must move on, no matter what the outcome. The only good thing that happened today is that I had three men look at my profile on my dating service, and they all seemed interested in me. Any person going through a divorce needs to feel special especially by the opposite sex, or they seem to feel unwanted— just a victim of their own failure. Why does it have to be that way? Why must one feel special while the other one feels like crap? It can never be fair; no matter how you look at it. I guess each person is in a different state in his or her life, but just knowing someone is there for you is the best medicine. I guess it doesn't matter if you are the victim or you are the adulterer, another warm body just being there is totally necessary. I need that feeling now, just as he has it in his life.

Well, dinner went ok. My son's grandma, yes, my soon to be ex-mother-in-law paid for the meal and even gave me cash as a present. I was surprised. The meal was fine too, and when my son went to the bathroom, I informed her that my son thought that his dad's new girlfriend was pregnant because they were having sex a lot. Her head immediately lowered, and she said that this would be the last thing that they would need. Finally, this expression of hers finally gave me an answer to the question that was bothering me. I had wondered for months what she thought of this situation. Now, I knew she was as disgusted as I am feeling. She's now in her 70s and her generation didn't believe in divorce, so they just stuck it out no matter how miserable each person had become because this social behavior was not tolerated. So, why is it so acceptable now? Maybe we just got smarter, or are we allowed to express our feelings more freely now?

Earlier in the day before this dinner, my son told me that his grandma said she was very sad about the conversation he had about his dad's girlfriend, and then she asked him to apologize. After we left the restaurant, my son and I talked about these comments. I asked him if he wanted to apologize for thinking she was pregnant. He told me no, and I informed him that if he apologized and he wasn't sincere, it's almost like a lie. I told him to do as he feels. I don't want him to pretend that what they did was ok. For, deep in his heart, he is very hurt by his dad's actions in addition to being confused and then acting upon his emotions. I mean, did she really think that her now "perfect" life would continue without any emotional baggage? She must be an idiot if she thinks that way. Maybe, I'm just too much of a realist, and they're living in a fantasy world? For their sake, maybe reality will hit them hard, and I mean so hard they wonder if their relationship was worth all the grief they've caused so many people.

As I woke this morning I had one thing in mind—she has feelings! I just can't believe she said that my son hurt her feelings! Hello? Where has she been this whole time? Is she stupid, or did she think that no one but her has a heart? Or, is reality striking at her now? Did he paint the picture that I was such a horrible person that she took pity on him and decided to have an affair? I am so dumbfounded that, a female, in particular cannot grasp how much it hurts when they put a knife into the heart of another female when she fools around with her man! Whether or not the road was rocky, between a couple or not, you just don't do that to another human being! Does she think it's ok with me since I haven't communicated with her yet? Everyone around me can see her actions as disgusting and deplorable. Maybe reality has set her thirsty eyes upon her life now and she will see the evil of her ways? At this point, I don't think she will, but only time will tell. But, I am sure of this—my son knows the truth about what happened, and I'm sure he will make her life a living hell, or at least come close with his angry comments. He's allowed to speak his mind—he's hurt and should be able to express his opinion. Right?

It's September 2, and my ex comes back from his hunting trip today. I'm sure I'll hear something about her and what my son said. I'm going to be honest with him and say my son has asked a lot of questions, and I have answered them to my best ability. What comes out of his mouth is beyond my control if he is acting on the facts. He's a teenager, and he will voice his opinion with or without my permission. Maybe my ex needs a reality check too. It will be interesting to see what happens in the coming days and months. Will they make it together based on their past history? If the both of them think marriage is hard, now they both have a chance to figure out if an affair is easier. The history of most people who have cheated doesn't make for a lasting relationship. But, who knows? Maybe they'll prove me wrong. But I do know this, something is definitely lacking in both of their lives, so they have to take from another life to make themselves feel whole again. On the other hand, I am feeling more secure with myself lately, but I do have days that I wish I could forget.

Well, it's one day after my birthday and more bad news; it seems to be following me everywhere. I went to my doctor, of whom I've known for almost 10 years, and his wife of almost 25 years just asked for a divorce. Is there a trend here? Did my ex start something that won't stop for a very long time? Where is that gasoline trail going next? Once again, that horrible feeling in my stomach has come back with a vengeance. He is devastated, and just couldn't stop talking abut the things that were going on and what she was doing behind his back. We even compared both of our situations. We both had spouses who took their vows and threw them out the window. They now mean nothing. All those years of commitment, the children, the lies and the deceit—what were the two of them thinking? So many people are affected when someone cheats! Are they so narrow-mind that they have tunnel vision? I really think so. In addition, I recently found a survey on why husbands cheat. Well, they do it for various reasons such as a lack of a sexual satisfaction or for someone younger, etc. Also, if you look at the headlines lately you'll see men who make a lot of money and have a lot of power who think they are above the laws of marital bliss. Do they think they won't ever get caught? Or, will their spouses just look the other way when the gig is up? Another reason seems to be that the "cheater" wants to feel better about him or herself, and they think they can find it in another person. Where does this new ambition start? Sometimes they forget why they were even in a relationship from the start. Our emotions seem to get in the way of our faithfulness to our spouse. I think my ex really did start off a friendship with her. But, after a while, I believe their friendship developed into a deeper passion and lust for each other that neither one of them really realized until it was too late. Then our relationship got pushed to the side and when he had to come home to me, it was anger that he felt because he was with me and not her. His heart had changed its mind about us being together because now he longed for another person's heart, and perhaps, bed. Maybe this is what was so hard for me to comprehend. Putting oneself in a situation with another who can comfort us, makes us feel good about ourselves and a feeling of calm, is what I think makes us want to go over to the other side. It's very easy when a spouse is where they seem to be comfortable and then they don't want to leave. Now, that the damage has been done, the mess is so great and it is too hard to clean up the pieces. But, it's as if they don't care, or if they do, the care and concern isn't on their shoulders. Now, it's me who no longer exists, and it's me who needs to be comforted. So now I have to be stronger than ever before. I mean, who really created this spilled milk, or did we all? This affair has to be cleaned up as much as it can, but the milk will sometimes always be spilled—sometimes forever.

That sick feeling is still there today, especially when I told my friends about my doctor's predicament and then saw their disgusted reaction. I don't think I have any good news to tell anyone anymore. Next, my son's Grandma called me to say she couldn't find my son to take him to school. Well, duh, he is at his dad's place and my son got confused and told her the wrong information. So, of course, it's my fault as usual. Since "he" doesn't communicate with his mom, I have always been the go-between and I guess I still am. My ultimate wish is that his mom treats "her" as well as she does me in that respect. Does she really know what she's asking for by being with him? The honeymoon will be over soon; I'm sure. I just want to stand by and watch.

Sometimes you wonder why life has to be so hard. Plus, at this particular time, why does it seem like not only is my life in turmoil, but everyone else around me is losing their family life too. This is too exhausting. I need a break. This weekend is Labor Day so I have to do something for me, maybe relax? That would be a novel idea. But knowing myself as I do, I'll have something to do—like take my vehicle in and have it checked out since my trip is next weekend.

On another note, a male co-worker and I, talked about the divorce madness that is now commonplace. He said that people do not even try anymore in a marriage. We have become such a disposable society, and it's too acceptable for one to just throw away plastic bottles as easily as their commitment to marriage. What have we become that relationships are as useless as tin cans? There's no "stick-to-itiveness'" in anything anymore. So, in regards to commitments, it's funny how songs can make you

207

think about your current situation. When I left my doctor's office the other day, the song, "It Must Have Been Love," came on the radio. I was driving and it took my attention off the road for a brief second.

The part that bothered me was the next line, which said, "… but it's over now. It must have been good, but I lost it somehow." This song was in the movie, *Pretty Woman*. In this movie, she wanted more than just a one-night affair and he couldn't commit to a relationship. The only difference between their relationship and my own, is that I was in a marriage that went array. My ex had serious commitment issues in general, he realized them and then he cheated. So, what makes a commitment stick? Who really knows the answer? All I know is that it's got to include respect and trust for the other person. I believe that both people need to compliment each other, and not one person trying harder in the relationship than the other. Our disposable society has made it ok to toss away material things as easily as they do people from their lives.

CHAPTER 12 →

Here We Go

*I*t's Saturday again. I'm at the point where I don't know how many weeks it's been since I found out his secret. I'm still not convinced if it really matters anymore? I'm having so much trouble sleeping that I can't even keep track of anything except the hours of sleep that I don't get. Too many things are still rolling around in my head. Maybe it's because "D" day is coming. Other things such as the other divorces and affairs going on around me, also disturb me greatly. I've even thought about writing a letter to her describing what she did to my family and me. But, what good would it do now? Would my life go back to being "normal" if I did? Besides, what is normal at this point? Would I want my life back as I knew it then? Probably not, but if it did, I'd really be miserable. I like my life as it is now. I mean, I've been able to do some of things that I've wanted to do for a very long time. I'm even buying the furniture that he would never let me purchase, because he wanted to make all the decisions on what we would get. On the other hand, my son is still resolving his emotions, and my life has had so many twists and turns that have affected every part of me, that I'm an emotional wreck. Some days I'm better than others, but lack of sleep is my problem now. Maybe I'm worried that I've made too many wrong decisions thus far. I've changed some monetary decisions and investments—and I did it all at once. For example, there is an office wall unit that I've always wanted, and my ex would never let me have it—well, it's being delivered today. The last time I bought new furniture, my bedroom furniture, it was only about a month ago and now there's more coming! I deserve it, damn it. I have felt so deprived for so long that it's my time to shine. Plus, I found out later that my neighbor "smiled" on my new decision about the new furniture— she commented to her husband that I was getting "his stink" out of my house. I thought that comment was funny, but it is quite true. In a way, I guess I am doing this for me more than anyone else. More than that, I'm getting his bad memories out of "my" house. Also, I am so amazed how calm and soothing the master bedroom feels now. I walk in here to retire for the night, and I can breathe again. I now feel it's mine. That's right—mine! This is a sanctuary that I deserve. In addition to changing the furniture, I again talked to a guy yesterday who works for a mortgage firm for advice on what to do with this house. I told him my situation and said that I don't have to sell, but I wanted him to see what's out there now, and if it is in my best interest to get into a different property. I just have to get my feelers out there to proceed with my next steps.

Things are still developing, and there is no definitive answer to my life right now. Only time will tell me the outcome. I think the part that bothers me more is that the loneliness is always staring me in the face. I miss having a hug from a man who wants to be with me. That passionate kiss, the look that could melt butter, and caring and concern is all missing in my life. I guess it was missing for several years in my marriage and I didn't know it was even gone. Somehow it snuck away and I was blinded by its absence. There are too many things to get a hold of for just one person, and to grasp it all at once is overwhelming. I guess it's like the old saying, "How do you eat an elephant?" The answer to that question is, "one bite at a time." This analogy seems a little stupid at this moment, but it's very true.

Today, the next change in my life came—my wall unit was delivered. I also cleaned the carpet in the entire house. Here was another feeling of success; more of his dirt was eliminated. It was January when I had last cleaned the carpet, and I had only done it then because we had to put our dog down. He was very sick and

211

was having accidents in the house constantly, so it was hard to end his life, but it was time to say goodbye. It was very tough to lose a part of "our" family, but it was necessary. As I look back now, this was probably the beginning of our roller coaster ride into the next phase of our lives. This event put another nail in the "divorce coffin" for us. We had gotten our dog as a puppy, but that was in happier times, and now the emotions between us and for our dog were changing and not for the better. My son was devastated that our dog was gone, and with that in mind, I'm sure the divorce was something that let go of his happier times too. Plus, my son thinks I'm still ruining the house by adding new furniture once again. Part of me wants him to get over his attitude that my life should stay the same and never change. It's ok for his dad to move on, but he doesn't want me to move on or even change one part of my life. I think he's so insecure with our split that something in his life desperately needs to stay the same. His dad now has what he wants—I don't think that I'm out of line by wanting my life to be better too. After this purchase, I think I'll slow down. If my son can get used to the current changes, perhaps the next change won't be as bad?

It's Sunday and church today was quite interesting—with one line of the sermon in particular. A line that said, "God will light your way." Well, little did I know that my day would end with a "hit" on my on-line dating service? I just happened to be on-line when a guy from out of state said hello. Well, we talked for two hours. The conversation was a little intense at first. He told me that he was a widower, and it sounded like he recently ended a relationship where his ex cheated on him. Little did he know it, but we both have really tender feelings right now. We talked about long-distance relationships and if I wanted to go any further since he was so far away from me. I told him that I really didn't mind and that I didn't play games. I'm too old for that crap! Especially now since my ex pulled that one on me. As each message went back and forth, we both seemed to open up a bit more. It's been so long since a guy was nice to me. For the first time in a long time, I feel special to someone. I know it seems a little quick, but, WOW, he sounds real. He seems genuine! I don't even know what his voice sounds like, but his words are so comforting. My 19 years of marriage didn't make me feel the way he did in two hours of chatting back and forth. He has a son like me, but much younger. Do I trust my feelings? How cautiously do I tread? He knows that I have an ex, but he doesn't know that it isn't final yet. Do I tell him? Or, does it really matter at this point in time? I'm probably pretty safe, because in 16 days, I will be the newest member of that club called, "The Divorced Woman's Society."

This is a very strange time of my life. I have such mixed emotions about everything. I want to be happy, but it's like wanting to learn to swim. I'm more afraid of drowning than making it to the other side of the pool. How do I proceed? Now would be a great time for a light to be turned on so I can see my new path. We even talked about religion. He said he was Catholic and had to go to church everyday when he was growing up. He was burned out with religion at this point of his life, and rightly so. I told him about my church, and how laid back and non-threatening it was. I don't think I've ever been so comfortable with church as I am right now. We are both spiritual, and I hope that will continue, because I have to have someone in my life that sees God as an important part of their life. I am supposed to talk to him tomorrow at 1 p.m. I can't wait to talk then. Will we make a connection? Who knows, but at least we got the formalities out of the way—our emotional baggage.

Last night's conversation with a complete stranger made me feel really good. Imagine that! Here is a man who is caring and compassionate and likes my picture. Where did he come from? It's as if he was sent to me from above. I'm still a little skeptical. Just call it erring on the side of caution. The ink isn't even dry on the divorce papers and I'm already infatuated with his picture and his words. I guess I'm a little out of practice with this dating game. Part of me is thrilled, but the reasonable side of me is unnecessarily cautious. I've heard of some people who really play with other people's emotions on-line and then manipulate them in different ways to their advantage. I have to be really careful with this relationship. Although I've "known" him for less than 24 hours, he seems authentic, but only time will tell.

It's like I'm in my 20s again and the world is at my feet. The only difference is that I'm older now, and hopefully wiser. At least I hope so. I now know what I want in a guy and I won't compromise any more. He has to respect women and cats, but first and foremost have God as Number One. My ex didn't have these traits at all. If he had respected women and worshiped, I'm sure we'd still be together. I only hope his new chick will figure this out before it's too late. It sounds like I feel sorry for her—well, maybe. I just know him too well, and I know he will never change. The chaos in his life will continue unless he doesn't cure his ills.

Well it happened—another guy who said he wanted to know more about me, stood me up online. I guess you could call it being stood up; he wasn't on-line when we agreed. Did I miss the communication hotline? I hope not; he seemed like he was interested. My ex did the same to me when we first dated. He said he would call me on a certain day, but waited until the next day to call. He said that he had company and it would have been rude to go off and call me when his friends were at his home. Well, what about me? If a person said they were going to do something— then do it! If you can't do what you're going to do, then don't bother me. I don't have time for people who lie. That old feeling from days past is what I now feel. It's a feeling of sadness; you know that feeling—the one where you've been dumped when you were sure there was something there. Maybe I'm wrong to suddenly judge another man. Maybe the hurt is too recent to move on. I thought I had a grip on life right now; perhaps I was wrong.

Well I was wrong about this guy. I did find him again on the Internet. We talked again for almost two hours. Where did this man come from? He says God brought us together. He's even e-mailed me the last two mornings. Is he as struck as I am? He is my waking thought and the last thing I think about when I go to sleep. I'm even waking up in the middle of the night and there he is again in my head. I've only known him for two days, but wow! Is he for real? Gosh, I hope so, because he has given me hope in men once again. If this goes the way I want it, he may be the one that I've waited all my life for. He's even talking about coming out here to see me at the end of the month. When he suggested that, I was a little taken back, but as I thought about it, I really want to meet him in person. Boy, has my life changed this year. It started off with issues with my son's school, my husband leaving, and now this new man who has swept me off my feet. I don't want this dream to end badly. It's like I need a crutch to keep me upright and standing, or even being at the bottom of a roller coaster. Can I deal with the ups, downs, twists and turns that keep hitting me in the face? Can I hang on when the ride drops 100 feet straight down or as it slowly climbs up to the sky? My stomach will tell me

I'm sure, because right now I'm very shaky.

All day, I was looking forward to talking to this new guy. I'm having a hard time believing he's real. I want to feel so much, but I'm a little reserved right now. I guess he is too. Every time I bring up the fact that I'd love to hear his voice, he relents. What is he waiting for? Is he uncomfortable on the phone? Will I think less of him for some reason? Or, is he hiding something? He did say he printed off my picture and put it in his bedroom and also used it as his screensaver on his computer. That action took me back a few steps. Some of the things he's done were rather quick and other times he's very reserved. How would I know these things? I've only known him for three days? It's like what a girlfriend in college said to me once, "I'm in like, not love." What the hell does that mean? Who knows, but I remember her eyes lit up and a smile surrounded her entire being. Even my girlfriend, whom I spoke with this evening, said that this entire ordeal has set me free. She said that I had a "calm" surrounding me now. I told her that I was really happy with my life since he left. I feel freedom, calm, and a sense of myself that I had not felt in many years. I also have a really romantic guy in my life that is very kind and caring—even if it is over the Internet. After tomorrow I won't be able to communicate with him for almost three days because of my trip. At this moment, it feels like an eternity. Why does this guy have such a hold on me? I can feel myself falling for him and

217

hard—this is way too fast—perhaps a rebound relationship? My co-workers even gave me the "thumbs up" when I showed them his picture. He was a little embarrassed when I told him that. I think I will give him my phone number tomorrow, and let him decide whether or not to call me while I'm on my vacation. I'm not sure this relationship will work, but I have to try and get back out there and play the field. Planting the seed will be my first test to see if this will last. I really like him, but my heart is very vulnerable at this point in time. Does he like what I say to him in our e-mails? Maybe. It will be interesting tomorrow to see what he says back to me. I really need to know what will be his real intentions in the coming days. He did tell me that his son has asked about me and he told him that I was the one who made him smile. I talked earlier about my son and how little boys just love their moms. His response was that one day his son might call me mom. Hello! This guy is really desperate or he's falling fast, and I haven't even met him in person yet! It's like he wants to open up, but his past hurt and anger about failed relationships is holding him back. What will I do with him? I just wish he lived closer; a hug would be really nice right now.

I hope this dream doesn't end soon. I'm really more involved than I want. Or, am I just a puppet who is being manipulated at this point of my life? I am really vulnerable right now and past relationships that end badly can happen to anyone, and right now it's my turn. He says he would never hurt me, and he doesn't believe I would do the same to him. I pray that we are meant to be together. He's on the East Coast, and I'm in Colorado; were our paths were meant to cross? The future is ours to continue the course. God, please make this dream a reality. I think I'm finally happy in a relationship, or is this just a bad dream just waiting to happen?

Our conversation had to come to an end earlier this evening. He was tired and I had to pick up my son from karate. His little guy is in kindergarten; so just a few years younger than mine. I remember when my son was that young. He was a little ball of fire. His energy kept me hopping, and I had trouble keeping track of him for the most part. All of his activities in school, and all of the little skits for Thanksgiving and Christmas were exhausting. Even Kindergarten graduation was a big deal. This part of their lives molds them so much. Part of this time cannot be taken so lightly. Just like a relationship, words and actions are the key if it works or if it doesn't work. I want to be happier than I've even been—that's my goal and I will have it. After writing these notes, I was missing him. So, I got on the Internet to e-mail him and something strange happened. When I started typing his name from my e-mail account, his last name was different than the dating service. I was a little taken back. Did he do this on purpose to hide his identity?

Many doubts crossed my mind, and that horrible little devil called suspicion raised its evil little head once again. All of a sudden, I got scared and my feet weren't moving fast enough to get away from my future. I had to e-mail him back. I didn't want to know the answer, but I bravely sent a question to him asking his reason for the two different names. He denied it emphatically, and that he wasn't out to hurt me. So, what do you call this? All of that trust I thought I had taken out of the closet—what do I do with it now? Am I just going overboard? Over reacting? Confusion is more my answer now. Does he not to want to talk to me because I will, point blank, ask a question and he will be on the spot with no where to run? So far in our conversations, he's been a little conservative in some of his answers. I can't wait until tomorrow to see his answer. I hope it is a good one.

Boy, all day I was livid. Did I meet another lying, cheating bastard so soon? I was just fuming all day. He never e-mailed me this morning, so is he now avoiding me? I don't know, but I'll find out soon. This day never seemed to end and still at 4:30 p.m. when it was time for me to leave work, I still had work to do. So, it was almost 5 p.m. when I finally left to get my son. Well, his dad had picked him up already so it was back to the grocery store to get food for the girls…a.k.a, my son's guinea pigs.

I brought some things in from the car and then headed straight upstairs. When I got to my computer, there he was waiting for me on the other end. We chatted for a while about the confusion, and it seemed strange about the two different names, but I bought his explanation. I hope his explanation is true, but why would he lie? Then, I did it, I asked for his phone number. He actually relented and gave it to me. Well, it was just my luck; I couldn't get through, so I let him know the issue. We tried it again and again—nothing. The next time was the luck I needed—I got through. So, now there he was, accent and all! My knees were buckling. Wow, what a sexy vice! Whew! There I go again, falling for a man who may be in my life forever. We only talked for a few minutes, and then we went back on line to finish our conversation. It was an hour later that seemed to fly by, and then we said goodnight. I had requested some pictures of him and his son. Within minutes, there they were in my e-mail account. Now I was in a serious state of "like." You know, that state of total infatuation that makes your entire body tingle? I think I've hit the jackpot! This guy makes me feel like nothing I've ever felt before. He even has, what he calls, a Belgian accent. To me it sounds more like a French accent. He told me that he knew French and would teach me. Funny how that works; I took French in high school, used it once when I went to Quebec and Montreal, but thought it was a useless to me ever since. Little did I know it would come in handy later in life? This divorce thing and now this new relationship has had my life up and down so much, it's no wonder that I have trust issues with men. This new situation feels like a dream. How did I get to this point in my life? It's interesting how so much strife can end up in a new beginning. Please, don't let anyone wake me up because I'm having the time of my life right now. But, now I've had two weird things that happened. First the two different last names, and now the phone issue. It's a little unnerving, but I'm still going to try to trust him; I hope I'm not chasing after another idiot who likes to lie to me!

The light at the end of the divorce tunnel must be a happy one because I even had a co-worker comment that she just loves her ex-husband. He gave her back her freedom and now she's in love with a new man and having a great time. Plus, Mary's getting stronger mentally, even though she's still having issues with her husband. I really believe he doesns't have a plan to on how to continue his life and is striking out at her to make himself feel better. It seems like he is grasping at straws to see how many he can get, so his life can progress faster than hers. It's almost like a game with him. I hope she can get to the point where I am currently. I'm really starting to feel the happiest that I've ever been. Nonetheless, I really wonder if I should be afraid of my future. Is this feeling really real? Should I be skeptical of my feelings? Well, my guard is still up, but I like what I feel right now. The days ahead will tell me how to proceed with my life.

It's September 10—the first day of my vacation. Of course, I woke up again—this time at 2 a.m.—big surprise! Instead of worrying about my future, I was thinking about the new man in my life. After an hour of not being able to get back to sleep, I got up and got onto my computer and sent him an e-mail. What is this hold he has on me? I haven't had that happen since I was engaged to my first fiancé and that was years ago. It was 1980, and I was just 19 years old. I was getting out of boot camp and had met him over a weekend when I was on Liberty. I fell hard and fast for him. He was eventually stationed in California while I was in Virginia. It was about a year later that he ended up cheating on me and eventually on the lady he married. I guess I had a habit of picking men who are dishonest and with wandering eyes. I hope this new guy isn't that way. He is, by the way, in another state so therein lay my caution. I want to go full force and tell him how he makes me feel, but I am hesitant to do so at this point. He, on the other hand, after five days says he loves me. This man is in love with our conversations and my voice! I haven't even seen him in person, nor have we held each other! Is he crazy? But, I want to be with him more than anyone else right now. Just his words make me melt. If he turns out to be as romantic on-line and on the phone as he is in person, watch out, I'm a goner! I so want to see him in person. I'm really looking forward to the day when I can look in his eyes because then he will be real. I've needed so much romance in my life and for years, I haven't had it at all. I was totally reminded of the "romance" thing this morning when my son's dad picked him up for their camping trip. All my ex could do was to, once again, complain how his truck was falling apart. So, he wasn't using his truck for the trip; he was using "her" SUV. I really wonder if he believes that this is the way things should have ended up? He has her to support him financially since his business is slacking. He once told me that if I had made a lot of money, that he would stay at home and be a stay-at-home dad. Seriously? I never believed that for a moment; he wasn't the type of person to do housework and take care of our son.

As for me, I'm worried about my future, and myself but it's becoming clearer; I hope. At least those are my thoughts for now. However, my son isn't happy at all about both of us finding other soul mates. I guess it is really happening too fast for his little brain to put the pieces together. But, the alternative isn't any better. When his dad and I were together, all we did was fight or ignore each other. So, which is worse? Both of us want to be happier than we were, and that means we can't be together—ever! I know that my happiness meter is in full throttle right now. It might take some convincing, but maybe my son will come around. I have to get him into counseling soon; he needs it right away!

CHAPTER 13 —

Looking Back; Moving Forward

Well, my vacation is definitely what I have needed. After a four-hour drive, I am here. First, I visited four wineries, and after tasting several different wines, I realized that I should have had lunch. After drinking, what amounted to less than one glass of wine, my body was numb but I was enjoying myself. So, it was off to get a salad and check into my hotel room. I didn't realize how exhausted I was from those hours on the road, but all the way there, I had thoughts of my new guy. Every song that once made me cry now had a different and significant meaning. There were a lot of lyrics about feelings, emotions and letting go so that one could start to love again. I think someone was telling me something about my new life, and I definitely needed to listen.

In addition to my life-changing experiences, my son told his dad that I had a boyfriend. I'm sure "he" is curious who he is, where he's from, and how I met him. That's probably the topic of their conversation today while they are driving to their campsite. My ex was shocked when our son told him, because he wanted to know if my new guy was going with me on my trip. Why does he care what I do now? Well, if he wants any details, he won't get them from me! Ha! It's interesting to me that what he does now with her, really doesn't affect me the way it used to. I have more things that I want to do and people I want to spend time with, than contemplating on his life. It's taken me a while, but now I'm better; the healing process is definitely taking hold in my life.

It's September 11, and another sleepless night. Although I went to bed last night at 8 p.m., it's now 3:26 a.m., and I'm wide awake for the "umpteenth" time in the last few weeks. I just can't sleep—I'm really tired of this crap! I'm happy, confused, or thinking about my life at its current state. I'm so perplexed about how my life is gong to turn out. It seems like I had it already figured out, then someone threw me a curve ball and I didn't know how to catch it. But now I have a new guy in my life, or do I? I can't get in touch with him today, and it's really bothering me. His phone is not working once again—another sign? It's amazing how many thoughts go through your head when just one little thing throws you for a loop. This relationship seems to be heading on a fast track to nowhere, and I've only known him less than a week. I haven't even seen him in person, but I wonder what it would be like to meet him for the first time. Am I kidding myself? Will this even work? There are too many emotions that will occur if this doesn't work. It's like a fairy tale—you know, the one that goes like, "boy meets girl; they fall in love, and they live happily ever after." Can fairy tales come true? It seems too hard to believe in any fairy tale right now. He seems so real, but so far away at the same time. He has touched my heart in a way that no man has done in over 20 years. I want to feel more, but something inside of me is holding me back. This feeling is telling me to be very cautious around him. I feel like I'm over reacting, but maybe its just jitters? He scares me, but at the same time he pulls my heartstrings. I want to be with him so bad that I can't sleep, nor can I eat. Needless to say, I've lost 16 pounds thus far during my newest crisis. At least one thing in my life is going the way I want. I keep praying for answers. I guess more time needs to pass before I can write the ending of my story.

My end seems to be coming sooner than I thought. He called me this morning at 6:30 a.m. I must have fallen asleep after my earlier sleep deprivation because all of a sudden my phone started to ring. It was a call that wakes you up and you're really groggy, and you're not sure where you are at that moment. However, it was a call that I needed to take. There he was at the other end of my phone! Those schoolgirl feelings just shot through my body at the sound of his voice. I was so happy to hear from him since I couldn't talk with him yesterday. The number I called didn't work and when he called me, he couldn't get through either. We only talked for a few minutes, but he made me laugh. He then proceeded with the comment that he likes to make me smile. Boy, does he ever make me smile! He even asked if he should get a hotel room, when he comes to see me. I told him that I wanted him to stay with me. That was what he wanted to hear, but I couldn't believe I was saying those words. He's convinced me that he's real, and he's also bringing his son, and I definitely want to meet them both. My son will definitely not like this, so I'm going to have them stay the week when my son is not with me. He's already having issues dealing with everything—this would set him off in the deep end—I just know it! This new relationship is happening fast for me too, but it feels right. I want it, and I definitely deserve some happiness! However, my gut reaction still haunts me and makes me wonder if I can really trust him. Is he real, or is he leading me on? I have to be on guard at all times now.

Another significant point, today is September 11—that I cannot overlook is that's its a day that will live forever in our history books.

A day that made Americans' realize what can be lost forever, and to value what we have. I remember it so well. A co worker and I were at work before 7 a.m. that fateful morning. Then, before we knew it, the radio had informed both of us of the event that rocked New York City. Then, we both consoled one another after this story began on that fateful day. That time was scary, and so many things have changed since then. Now it's my life that is scary, because I don't know the changes that will occur in my future—whether they will be good or bad. I mean, go figure, little did I know where I would be today, for I am on vacation by myself and I'm having a great time! I don't think I ever wanted to go somewhere by myself, let alone a vacation. But, today, I went site seeing and then to visit more wineries. After relaxing for a while this afternoon, I'm headed to the Hewy Lewis concert, and yes, by myself! Tomorrow I will return home with wine, a box of peaches, and some presents. I bought my son and his son a souvenir. Do I really believe that he will come to visit? In my heart I do; I just hope it comes true. I guess I need something to break the ice at the airport when I pick them up. The more I think about it, the more nervous I'm getting about meeting them both. He seems to have fallen for me with just a picture and our conversations. What will he think of me when he meets me for the first time in person? I'm nervous and excited all at the same time. I want to be with him in the worst way. If this is love, I'll know when I first meet him. Those butterflies just don't stop fluttering just because I'm not near him.

It was midnight when I got back from the concert. This group was awesome! I now know why he's been around for so long. Some of his band members have been with him for over 10 years. They even seem to have fun doing what they do best and they are so committed to each other—so many people can learn from these guys. Perhaps that's why he seems so comfortable in his own skin. There are so many men out there who can't say that, or even know how to treat people. It's funny how every little thing makes me think of my impending divorce. I don't think I've made this much effort to compare things in my life that needed to be analyzed. But, I think it's a good thing to do, so that I won't make the same mistakes again in a new relationship.

I wasn't gone for long on my trip, but on the way back I had a lot of time to contemplate. Once again, every CD that I played seemed to talk about love and relationships and how things can be good or bad. With my four hours of sleep from last night, and driving back home, it was a lot to think about. Where did he come from? Because, all of a sudden he entered my life and took a hold of every emotion that exists in my being! I want to feel more for him, but there are so many questions that I have with no current answers. I barely know him and he wants me to say that I love him. I can't do that yet; I'm just not ready. I can't give up my newly found freedom that seems so open to new possibilities. If he is real, I will never let him go. If he isn't, where do I go from here? I mean, I'm having trouble calling him on his phone—why? Is he who he really says he is? I mean he wants to come out to stay with me. Am I crazy for saying, yes? Am I asking for trouble? Why does life have to be so complicated? I know I'm not the only person who has met someone on the internet, but at this point, I don't have anyone really to ask about internet dating—at least the long-distance kind. I don't know where to go from here, especially, since I didn't get to talk to him today. Why is it that when I don't talk to him, I have some serious doubts? When I do talk to him, every care I have is taken away, and I feel his presence throughout my body. He knows just what to say to me that makes me feel safe. This journey seems to be getting more complicated, and not just the journey of driving home. I just need to know that the direction I'm going is the right one, but no one can tell me. There are no answers. I'll just have to figure out this one on my own. I've realized now that "Divorce," doesn't come with an owner's manual—it's a "pay as you go" adventure.

Once again, the next morning started off at 3 a.m. But, this time I was getting a migraine headache. Now, reality was setting in—no sleep and too much stress always gives me a headache. I took some of my medication and went back to sleep. After a few hours, I woke up and thought my headache was going to grow into something uncontrollable. My vitamins once again saved me. Then, after checking my e-mail, I had once again missed him. My 3 a.m. e-mail got to him, but the two-hour difference in time does mess with our communication. I also got onto the scale this morning and I have now lost 16 ½ pounds so far. My bad knee is even feeling better. Two torn meniscus should hurt a lot and before loosing that much weight, it really did. Life is getting better every day. I can't believe that I am happy again. Three months ago if someone would have said that life would be this good, I would have cried out loud with pain in my voice. Now, I have freedom to come and go as I please, I just went on a vacation, and I have met the most wonderful, romantic guy whom I thought did not exist. It's almost like I'm waiting for the bubble to burst—or will it?

My only problem is convincing my son that both of his parents are much happier apart, even though he doesn't think it is true. I tried telling him that his dad made me cry for many years, and that he did not respect me. He is dead set on not believing anything I tell him. He also still thinks that he has to keep an eye on his dad and his girlfriend and notate everything they do in a journal. Also, since my new guy wants to come here, my son refuses to have dinner with us. I have planted the seed for him to accept someone in my life; hopefully, he will come around. He won't be here for a couple of weeks, so maybe my son's mind can be changed. All I know is that my new love makes me appreciate life again. He makes me feel special and I need that so much right now.

It may sound strange, but I'm so thankful for my ex doing what he did. Although the way he did it wasn't pretty, he really did me a favor by leaving. Boy, I never thought I would ever say that! I even bought them both a bottle of wine while I was on vacation. I got home yesterday and today when I went to pick up my son from his house, I brought the wine and some other things over to my ex that he asked me to bring back from my vacation. Yes, believe it or not, I did that! Then, I went up to his house, walked in the door after my son, and handed him the bottle of wine. The words just seemed to flow out of my mouth as I had practiced. I said, "I bought you a thank you gift. Thank you for giving me my life back!" In the 19 years that I've known him, I have never seen him shut his mouth, look totally shocked, and then lower his head in shame. Score two points for me! The man was dumbfounded, and I was proud of myself for finally heading towards my independence from his reign. He didn't say two words after that one-way conversation. I just wonder if she heard me from another room utter those words. I wasn't being mean, just honest, for I meant every one of them. He really did me the greatest favor he could have ever done. I've gone from totally devastated to totally and disgustingly happy. I'm sure if he's out to get revenge for my actions, I'll hear about it tomorrow. I even told a co-worker, whom I saw later that day, of my comments and her reaction was priceless. She was really proud of me!

Today, I received a couple of e-mails from my new guy. His business plans are taking him to another country. He's having to "plane hop" several times to get to his destination. I've really thought a lot about him, and one of his e-mails said that he was lonely and that he missed me. He is so sweet in his e-mails; I just can't get over the words that he says to me. It's like being in a romance novel. This is happening all too fast, but it seems so real and so right. It reminds me of a guy that I was once engaged to years ago. That relationship started out quickly and lit up like a light bulb, but it died as quick as a clap of thunder. The only difference between these two is that I'm older now, and I'm more willing to grab hold of a relationship that I know is right. I want so much to see him in person—that will convince me it's not a dream. He just encompasses my every thought. How and why did I let him do that to me? The answer is not clear right now, but I intend to find out in a few weeks.

It's the 15th of September; just eight more days and I'm free from that horrible marriage. Also, in a few short weeks, my new guy will be here; I can't wait. Right now he's half way around the world on a business deal and will return home perhaps in the next few days. He even called me after we chatted on line. His voice is so sweet and kind—nothing like I've ever heard before. He lights up my world and it's hard to concentrate on anything else. Is this too early for me to feel this way? I still don't know, but I feel like a teenager again with my first crush. No one can compare to him—it just feels right. He's a 180-degree turn from my ex. He's kind, caring and very compassionate. Wow! I think I'm getting closer to the "Love Potion Number 9" bottle every day. Every time I see his picture, I take a quick, short breath and feel happier than ever before. I have to see him and it has to be soon.

It's another early morning—this time it's now 2:30 a.m. At least I'm waking up with a smile on my face now. I just lay there for an hour before I finally got up and then I had to e-mail him. It was only after that when I could get any rest. The alarm clock finally awoke me at 5:15 a.m., and my usual routine began all over. The only difference lately is that it's a lot easier to get through my days. There's hardly a minute that goes by that I don't think of him. There's such a bond between us, and we haven't even met in person yet. I keep saying that, but it's very true. My only concern is that I'm infatuated with someone I cannot even hold in my arms. Is this "dream" too good to be true? This Internet dating thing is definitely different—especially a long-distance one. I pray this relationship is permanent. There's just something about him that I can't lose.

Another day has passed and he is still in another country. Now, he's informed me that he lost his computer and his cell phone. He also called me several times this morning but I had my phone on my desk and not with me, while I was in another room at work. Finally a co-worker brought me my phone and said someone was really trying to get in touch with me. I had my phone in my possession for about two minutes, and it rang again; there he was! I'm not sure if he needed someone to complain to, or just needed to talk to me. We compared notes on the time of day, and I told him that I had only been at work for just an hour and couldn't talk. He told me of his difficulties of not having a computer because he couldn't buy a new one due to the retailer not taking his credit card. This should have been a BIG red flag to me, because I started wondering if he wanted me to wire him some money. I didn't know the answer, and didn't offer any. I refuse to start off a relationship with a money issue lingering over both of our heads. Maybe my instincts were starting to come out and that metal wall went up around me, because it scared me a little. I really don't know this guy at all! Perhaps this is a reality check—for I will not be taken advantage of this soon, maybe never. I feel good with him, but cautious at the same time. My trust in men is definitely on shaky ground. I want to be with a man again, but this romance thing is complicated sometimes.

That roller coaster keeps going up and down and I'm still on that front car—you know, the place where everything is hitting me in the face and I can't get a grip on reality. It seems as if life goes slow and then it speeds up so fast that I can't catch my breath. I'm getting really sick of this! I don't know what each day is going to bring because each minute changes. That sick feeling keeps me ill. I mean, I'm not physically sick—it's more of an emotional "gut wrenching" sickness. It's those emotions that can set you off into the deep end, and then you're drowning before you know it, then you can't come up for air? If I finally see him in person, maybe I could trust the opposite sex again. As for now, it's not quite set in stone. I need lots of prayers to keep my sanity.

Ok, now it happened. Day 8 of our relationship, and the bomb dropped. He said the retailer over there wouldn't accept his credit card—again, so he has now asked me for funds to help him buy a new one. One instant message chat got me a little more distant after he brought that up! I flat out refused, and thought he was scamming me. I wasn't going to let it happen to me. I immediately got off line and called my girlfriend. I told her what just happened and she was shocked. As we talked, I heard my cell phone ring, and then there was a beep on my house phone. I told her it was he, but I wasn't answering it. I felt betrayed once again by a guy that I let into my heart. How dare he ask me for financial assistance— he doesn't even know me! Those same familiar pains in my gut stuck out like a sore thumb. After my girlfriend and I compared notes for a while, I hung up the phone to ponder my next move. I went upstairs into the office and got onto my e-mail account. There, staring me in the face was a quick note from him asking why I didn't answer his calls. He, very subtly, stated that I meant the world to him, and how I really hurt him by giving him the cold shoulder. Did I do something wrong by not wanting to send my hard-earned dollars to a man I barely know? This guy said sweet nothings to me for several days and now it seems he wants to take me for what I'm worth and then take off! What person does this to someone so vulnerable? Who knows, but I was standing my ground, and my sword and shield were by my side. He scared me. I mean, he had said all of the right things to make me feel loved and very special. Now, he was going in for the kill, or at least this is what I felt. As I sat there and re-read through his e-mail, the phone rang once again. Before I could see the caller ID, I just knew it was he—and of course it was. He sounded very upset and sad. I had hurt him greatly, or this is what he said. I tried to explain why I did what I did. This relationship was only eight days long; not eight years, and men can manipulate vulnerable women to the point of financial loss. I told him I wouldn't let it happen to me. I also told him that my emotions were running high; I had been in a relationship where there wasn't a lot of trust for a very long time. We ended the conversation and I don't even remember the words we used. I just know I hung up the phone feeling very confused. If he were just after money, why would he continue in this romance? Or, was it a ploy to get back into my good graces? I don't understand. This is happening all too fast. I do remember telling him that he needs to do whatever he needed to do and take as much time doing it, as he needed. I wasn't in a hurry for him to get here that quickly. I tried to make it sound like I really cared and was sorry for jumping to conclusions. But, was I wrong? I'm protecting myself, and if that's wrong, then so be it! I'm a survivor and I'll do anything to protect my son and myself. My theory in life is, "Hell hath no fury, like a pissed off Mom," or in my case, "a pissed off ex-wife."

After talking to a girlfriend on the phone later on, she was totally confused as well. I asked her thoughts and she said to see what happens tomorrow. I had to let her go then; she had to make dinner and it was already 7 p.m. We would meet tomorrow for drinks, and then discuss this situation more. Because we are meeting, that will mean that I won't be home at 5 p.m. like I always am, so should I have told him this information or not? We'll see what e-mail response I get from him since I sent him one discussing my vulnerability to this whole mess. In addition to this new confusion, today makes the last week I'll ever have to say that "he" is my husband. Why is this all happening at once? I think I've been indoctrinated into the "Drama Queen Idiots" club.

CHAPTER 14 —

Changing Times

I woke up this morning just minutes from my alarm clock setting. For once I didn't do the 3 a.m. wake up call to myself. I'm not sure why I finally got the much-needed sleep that I've been deprived for weeks now. How did I do that? We had a big fight last evening, and now this relationship is just as traumatic as some of my fights with my ex. This new guy scares me a little. He's taking charge of this marathon relationship, while I am doing a slow crawl. Where are we heading? All I know is that his e-mail this morning was up beat and professing his affection and how he can't live without me. I'm so confused. Where do we go from here? I mean that's two strikes against him now—is this a sign that I should have been looking for from the start? I've tried not to base all relationships on the last, but really! Only time will tell I guess.

Yesterday was quite busy in addition to interesting, and I was looking forward to meeting Marie for drinks after work. We've met other times when we could, but it always seemed to be based on my schedule. Well, this evening was based on the conversation of last night. Call me cautious, but why would someone profess their love to you after four days, and then ask you for money after just one week? I mean, how much of an attitude do you have to have to do something that bold? I even checked my e-mail this morning, and now I had an amount that he wanted me to send him--$500. I have that much money, but why would I give it to someone that I have never met in person? Well, he doesn't know it, but there's a website that I checked out, and I have contacted them to see if this is really a scam. The first mistake this new guy made was to give me his "home address," so I went on-line to check it out. Well, guess what, his address is really a car dealership in New Jersey. Does he think I'm stupid? What a dumb ass! Or, is he giving me a line of bull? Well, you can't argue with a computer; at least I'm not; especially when it gives me a map. I'm not sure what I will do next, but I may ignore his request, and his calls. I need to put a plan in place and perhaps contact a local TV station to see if they can check out this scam.

I really didn't sign up for this part of my life, but, now that it's here, I have to be ready for the challenge. It seems like there's one thing after another lately and it's just too exhausting to continue. The only good news that I recently got is that my little sister is going to have a baby—I'm so excited for her! Years ago I remember her life was in such turmoil. Now it's my turn? What gives? I was having trouble concentrating, not because he engulfed my every thought, but now this relationship is probably a scam. So, I forwarded his latest e-mail to some of my girlfriends. They were all surprised and said to really watch him. I have decided to sit back and not answer the phone or any of his e-mails that I get from him. I refuse to let him abuse me in any way, I've had too many years of that crap already, and it won't happen again. Now, I'm stronger and I'm definitely working to separate my heart from my checkbook—little does he know I will not be taken advantage of in any way. I almost want him to be investigated. But is it worth it to have a background check done on him? Is it really worth my while? How much more effort do I need to put into this relationship before I just lose my mind? I'm not sure I really need that kind of closure. I guess it's common to have your heart touched so deeply by scam artists right after a divorce, but I'm older now and I refuse to let it happen to me. Don't get me wrong. I still have my membership to my on-line dating service, so that may be my next step to get back into the dating world and get rid of this jerk. I haven't given up on relationships, but my next step will be for me to tread a little lighter next time. My next relationship will NOT be a long-distance one—guaranteed

This dating thing was really lying heavy on my heart, so I decided to get onto a site that did background checks. The website that I found just gave a little more about a person that you're curious about. Well, the initial results made me think that I had found him. His first initial and last name matched with the city he said he lived in, but his average income and home value didn't fit, besides that burning feeling that his address was a car dealership made me really wonder now. This service was one that I paid for, but since it didn't cost a lot, it was worth it to find out a little more information. Now, I'm more concerned that this guy is phony. His profile is not matching his words.

Today is Friday, and five more days until "D" day. So much has happened these last three months, and I'm so distrustful of men in general. Besides, this new love interest still worries me. There are so many red flags with him. I even went home this evening wondering where we stood. What were his intentions? Was I supposed to be putty in his hands and melt every time I receive an e-mail or phone call? I know that I'm in the same boat as Mary who seems to be having some of the same problems. She can't hold her emotions together when her ex is around. He is so manipulative to her that she has a hard time holding her current life together without him. Her self-esteem and self-confidence is still very vulnerable. We talked for a while yesterday and she said that there's a very lonely part of her life that she still has to deal with.

Even though our circumstances happened within a week of each other, we are at very different levels with our loss. I have moved onto a view of "thanking" him. She has moved to a level of just coping. Three months is a very short time to deal with this "death" in our lives, and it will continue with or without our permission.

The day couldn't be over soon enough, but the end of the workday was finally here, and I was out the door. It took just under 15 minutes to get home, and my cat greeted me at the door, as usual. I immediately headed upstairs to the office to check my e-mail to see if there was anything new. His message this morning asking for $500 for a new computer was enough to set me off into the deep end. What did he want from me? Seriously, does he need a green card and has to marry someone to stay in the states? Is he taking me for a ride around the block and trying to get everything, financially and emotionally, from me? I feel that he is trying to drain me. My better judgment is now kicking in. As I sat at my computer, the phone rang and it was he. I didn't want to answer because I needed time to think. Since it was a long week, and I was really tired, I went to bed early instead of answering the phone. Well, the phone rang again at 11 p.m. Once again, I wasn't answering, because he had awakened me from a dead sleep and my concentration wasn't as good as it should at that hour. After a good nights sleep, I felt better. But, 5 a.m. hit and there went the phone again. Guess who? This time I did answer. He asked why he couldn't get me. I didn't want to tell him of my suspicions and concerns, so I told him that I thought I was getting sick, and I went to bed early. His comment was that he wished he were here to take care of me. Then, all of a sudden he said he couldn't hear me, and he had to pull over and call me back. Now I was really suspicious—didn't he tell me earlier that he had lost his cell phone in addition to his computer? So, whose phone was he using? I had more questions. I don't get it! Can I really trust his man? Am I crazy for even talking to him? Also, before we hung up he had asked if I had gotten his e-mail from yesterday. At first I thought he was talking about the one asking for money. Well, I said no, I hadn't gotten it. I had to go check. After we hung up, I went into my home office and got into my e-mail account. There was another e-mail from him. This time, as usual, he was professing his love to me, but at the end, was a statement he said that shocked me. He mentioned that although we have known each other for such a short time, he knew that I loved him and that everyone around us didn't believe it could happen as fast as it had for us. In addition, he mentioned what a good wife and mother I would make for him and his son. Is this guy flipping serious? I've known him for 12 days! I've never met him in person. I've only seen pictures, heard his voice, and read his e-mails. No wonder I'm running scared. I just don't know what to think now. At this point two hours had passed and I needed to feed my pets and get into the shower. He still hadn't called back, so I got ready to do some errands and to think things through without him.

Another day has passed and it was exhausting; it's just four days until "D" day. Plus, I got into another fight with this new guy. I didn't think new relationships should start this way, but this one has and I don't like it. He still wants me to give him a "loan" for the money he requests. He called me several times today to ask me for it. We finally got on-line and talked. Our conversation started off pretty casual, but it quickly was heated. Does he not know etiquette when it comes to asking for financial assistance? I've now known this guy for just two weeks, 14 days, and I can't consciously do this! I've said it before, I can't give money to someone I don't know. Hell, I can't even get myself to give money to people I've know for five years, let alone two weeks. Maybe I'm afraid that I'll be "screwed" once again by a man who's out to get me, or I'm not ready to get run through the ringer again. How or why should I trust him? I have no reason to trust anyone this fast. He seems so sincere, but how do I let him in, or do I? I don't even know what direction I should precede. I know I've upset him, and we had ended our conversation with him getting a headache from my refusal of his request. I really felt bad that told him my Irish/German temper was coming out and to not to tread on me. I guess I was just getting really upset that he wouldn't take "No" for answer. When I say "No," I really do mean "No." Boy, he's as stubborn as me! What will I do with him? If he's as sincere as he says, we'll make it through this mess, but if he's not, we're through.

It's Sunday now and he is still harassing me. He called me again, and the first thing out of his mouth was, "Are you going to help me?" Is he for real? I tried to stall and say I would have to think about it. Little did he know I was on a mission to destroy his little plan? After attending church this morning, I realized I was given the answer I needed—one must be a cheerful giver in life. This was the answer that I needed to hear and now I was confident as to what I needed to do. I had been really hesitant about sending him money, and today I had my answer from a higher authority that was looking out for me—I just know it. After church, I got another call from him, but I didn't answer my phone. I got the courage to send an e-mail to say I would not help him and that I had contacted the local law enforcement agency (of which I had), and he'd better leave me alone and get out of my life. He was old enough to get himself out of a jam and he needed to handle this himself. It was amazing how the phone calls and the e-mails stopped. How desperate did he think I really was for his romantic ways? Well, he didn't know whom he was dealing with—I'm not an idiot! No man will make me a fool of ever again—I hope!

My girlfriend, Jackie, who was also on the same dating site and I, compared notes on this situation. She was having some similarities with a guy she met too. There were too many similarities between the guys we were meeting—a guy with too many compliments, going overseas for a business deal, and a guy who wants to start his own business. I made sure she was aware that we're probably both being scammed, and to be careful—so now she has her guard up higher than before. Do these men know whom they're dealing with? My answer would be, "A Big Fat No!" We're not 18 years old; we're in our late 40s and wiser than these idiots think we are! What a bunch of dumb-asses! They just don't know the depth of our intelligence and that our years of knowledge have brought us this far in our lives.

Our only downfall may be that when we finally do meet the right guy, we may drive them away if we're too hard on them. If we find a guy who is willing to understand our needs and our past experiences, then and only then, will we get to the next good relationship that may last? If they understand and go slow in a relationship it may work; I'm ready for that, but I must proceed cautiously. Time will only tell. I've not given up on this on-line dating thing; I'm just more guarded now.

Maybe I just want some companionship since "D" day is in three days. Or was it that my son said today, when he came home, that his dad told his new chick that he loved her. This disturbed him very much. He also told me that he was very protective of me and that was why he didn't want me to date anyone. Our conversation was such that he had tears in his eyes and he was getting very upset. I could just see the stress in his very being. Especially, since I told him that the divorce was final on Tuesday. His dad would be free to marry her if he so chooses. I know this didn't go over well, and his emotional shield was completely surrounding him. I know his thoughts. He thinks his dad and I can still work out our troubles and come back together. Little does my son know that I wouldn't take his dad back if he were the only man left on earth! Sex isn't worth that much grief! We will never be "together" ever again! I don't want to tell my son that—he's just not ready to hear those words. So now I'm finally living a life worth living!

It's September 21; the 90th day after we first filed for divorce. Just today and tomorrow is all that is left of our marriage, and then I'll be joining that club with other divorcees who have gone before me. Besides, the ink isn't even dry on the papers yet and this new guy is on his way out. He just doesn't get the hint. What part of "go away" doesn't he get? For when I got on my computer this morning, there he was again. "Hello Honey!" was his comment. Well, that just about set me off once again. I deleted his profile and selected the spam key. Gee, I thought I was stubborn—good Lord, he's worse than me! The only thing he doesn't know about me is that I can be just as stubborn. I've just been cheated on by the Number One Bastard in the country and now he's been busted as a scammer, and, guess what, I won't be a victim again. I even got back onto the on-line dating service and saw another guy that was interesting to me. After checking my account, this guy has e-mailed me back. Guess where he is? Germany. Am I a magnet for jerks? It's beginning to make me wonder. I guess I can't judge all men like this first one, but that steel cage is closing in on me and I'm not getting out any time soon. It's not even 7 a.m. and I feel like I need a drink! Someone please pass the rum.

I'm even drawn towards Jackie's situation too. She met a guy on-line, and he's going to Africa soon on a business trip—sound familiar? We've gone back and forth on this issue for a few days now, and now she's really concerned. So far he hasn't done anything wrong, but she's very aware of what could happen. Needless to say, we've talked more in the last week than we have in a very long time. We're looking out for each other since both of our ex's, were and still are, very hurtful to us both. So, today, Jackie, and I are closely comparing notes. Her guy is sending her such heart-felt poems that she's a little disturbed. Six poems hit her cell phone within a 10-minute time frame. When we talked a few times today, each and every time things got a little more strange. Then, she got another bouquet of flowers with the same poem as the last arrangement. This time it was 24 roses, but

251

since the words reflected that they've known each other for only six days and the arrangement should have reflected six roses, her doubts about him grew stronger, because the last arrangement was six roses. So, in reality, she should have only gotten six roses—once again. Talk about another scam! Her first thoughts were that he had another woman whom he was stringing along, and he got them confused. This on-line dating thing is getting quite interesting.

It's September 22, 2009—the 91st day after we filed for divorce. "D" day is finally here. I don't have any regrets that it's finally the day; I'm just a little nervous how this will all play out. Today was the first day we could get a court date, so I guess today is it. Our appointment is at 4:30 p.m., and of course, I arrived first. I always got anywhere before him—it was his trademark to always arrive about one minute before anything ever happened. That used to drive me crazy, but I guess after today it doesn't matter any more. So, since the couple before us didn't show, the magistrate was ready earlier than she would have been. She even asked me if my "husband" knew what time to show up—I replied that yes, he's aware of the time. Well, at 4:27 p.m., the door opened up and there he was. We were asked to sit at the front tables, and raise our right hand to swear that what we were about to say was the truth. After each question she noted our replies to our agreements, and seven minutes later, we were a married couple no longer. Wow! There it was, seven minutes to erase almost 19 years of marital bliss—NOT! I mean, I was quite nervous about this whole process, but now I had my finality. She handed us a copy of the decree and now it was done. She also told us we could purchase a certified copy after the fact, but at that time, I didn't want to think that far ahead.

We walked out of the courtroom together, but now something was different. We weren't as one anymore; now, we were two individuals—single individuals—on our way to our new lives. How would our relationship be different now? I mean, we hadn't been together in the same house for three months, so I guess the only difference was that we both could have our own separate love lives now with only one thing in common—our son. We were free to marry, or date as we pleased. Boy, what a strange feeling! I wasn't sure what to do with my newly found freedom this soon. Even our conversation on the way out was very short and direct. We didn't linger outside and talk as we had when we initially filed. We parted ways and all we said to each other was, "See ya," then we both left in our own vehicles and in separate directions. There was a great emptiness that swept over me that confused my soul. I guess we were done with each other now—it was now final.

I immediately called a few of my girlfriends to tell them of my newly found freedom. They seemed happy for me, but I think they were truly concerned of what I would do next. I don't think they knew what to say to me for they were probably so drained from everything that I had laid upon them during this entire feat. He was probably now planning his next marriage ceremony—who knows, but did I care? All I knew was that there was a bottle of wine with my name on it awaiting my arrival at home. It was a bottle that I had opened last night and it was there for me, there for the taking. Plus, since my now "ex" mother-in-law was picking up my son from karate, I had the evening to myself—well, at least a couple of hours. The contents of that bottle went down too smooth with my leftover pasta from last evening. I wanted more wine, but I refrained. I needed to get in touch with my son, but I couldn't, because his grandma's home number wasn't working as I found out later. But, my son finally called me saying he'd be home soon. While awaiting his return, I even went onto the Internet and commented on my day in a blog. I received a message from my niece that her divorce was final on September 16. She had just filed on July 31! I guess the rules for divorce were shorter in her home state. In my state it's final in 90 days, but only if you agree on everything. I guess it's funny how things happen in life. I remember when she was born, and I watched her grow up from afar. When it was her turn to get married, I was so proud of whom she had become. Little did I know that she would marry a worthless, selfish man who controlled her every move and then cheated on her? But, now we're both better off. We both have our lives back—something we needed more than a man in our lives that made us miserable. Her marriage had lasted only three years; mine was almost 19. Now we share a common thread—a cheating, lying husband, scary, huh? Can we both sleep a little more sound now? Who knows? I just know I am wiser after this, and like this morning's e-mail from that bozo on the east coast, I will not put up with lies and deceit anymore! I might be a smart-ass sometimes, but I'm sure not a dumb ass by any means! I've lived years in just the last three months. I pray that I find my way soon—even if I don't find a guy to share my life with.

Well, it's not even 24 hours since the ink has finally dried on the divorce papers, and I'm doing my 2:30 a.m. wake-up call once again. My internal clock has got to be reset! But, since

I was up, I just had to check my e-mail account. Well, guess what? No new e-mails from that bozo from yesterday. I feel so empowered now, and I'm passing that strength onto Jackie who thinks her guy is a fraud too. I guess no news was good news and that made me go back to sleep quite easily. Now, it seems I can focus on my son and myself, but he is still very upset with this mess. He's still acting out by yelling at me for everything I do and say. I guess it's just his way of verbalizing his distrust of parents and/or adults in general and of our actions. I can't totally understand his viewpoint because my parents were never divorced; although, sometimes I had wished they were when I was younger. Arranging some counseling would probably help him at this point—it might even help me. He's so sad and confused. I don't know what to say to him and I don't think he'd listen even if the words came out of my mouth to comfort him. This next period of our lives will be a challenge; we must struggle through each day towards the healing process that we both need.

Today, I got several comments from my friends and co-workers. They showed concern, cheered my victory, and even said I was now part of the Cougar Club. You know, that club for divorced women over 40 who are after men younger than them? This is all so new for me. The only person still angry with me is my son. He wants to destroy everything new that I'm so desperately trying to accomplish. He's now trying to destroy the paint finish on the kitchen cabinets that I re-did. He wants them to return to the same color as before—perhaps if he accomplishes this, everything will return to his version of "normal." I can't let him destroy anything, and I am trying to correct his wrong with a change for my better and not his. I tried to get his attention by telling him that my doctor is also getting divorced. He was quite surprised at this news, for he knows him. I told him that my doctor is mad, confused, frustrated, and going through every emotion there is, but could not explain what he feels. He seemed to understand this analogy and said he agreed with what I just said because he was feeling the same way. I have to get him counseling soon. Maybe I'll go through my church. Something has to be done soon; he's hurting and I don't know how to handle this situation. No one ever gave me Divorce 101 lessons, so now I'm getting an "F" on my final trying to teach the same lessons to my son.

It's now Thursday; almost two full days of freedom have passed or something that resembles freedom. I'm well on my way to the next level of confusion because the fall holidays are very close. First, it's Halloween, then Thanksgiving, and finally Christmas and New Year's. This year it will be interesting on how I will deal with them. I've had a set routine for the last two decades, and now it has drastically changed. I no longer have a mother-in-law, and his sister, my ex sister-in-law, has also gone away in a flash. So, I don't have any family members who live close to me. These new thoughts can be overwhelming, but I can't dwell on them now. I can't lose the only sanity that I still have. I want to continue on with my life and hopefully be happy now. I don't know what will happen, but I'm sure it will be a rocky road ahead. It can't be smooth—I just know it!

Well, it happened, three days after the divorce and he started a fight. All of a sudden, everything I do is wrong, and everything he does is right. Go figure? He's such a hypocrite—he's now going to counseling and suggested that I do it too. Because, as he put it, "you have to fix yourself before you can fix anyone else." I think I've said "hypocrite" before, but now I mean it. He wouldn't go to counseling when we were having problems years ago, but now he's had an inspiration? Did a lightening bolt hit him in his ass or something? I mean, don't get me wrong, it's about time he's getting some mental therapy. He's needed it for years to fix what ale's him. His childhood has been a big sticking point for years now. He blames much of his failures in his adult life to that time period. I didn't have the best childhood either, but I try to see the positive features now, but he can't for some reason. Perhaps, his new "chickypoo" has given him inspiration to fix himself? Whatever made him go; I hope it helps. I don't totally hate him for what he did, although, I have reason to do so. I try to wish the best for everyone, especially, if they are hurting and need a new direction.

Well, my on-line dating thing is still alive and well. I met another guy online and he's doing business in Africa too. What is this "Africa" thing? Here's another situation where I'm going to tread lightly once again. There is so much to think about now. Even my doctor is still at a stand still. He and his wife are still having issues. I don't think that they will make it through their present state of affairs, and get back together. The trust they need is not in their relationship, and their financial issues are the hot topic between them. I feel like I'm in such a better situation than them; I'm free. No more husband to tell me what to do, and to make my life miserable. But, they're stuck in a marriage that is going nowhere fast. Even Mary is still dealing with her ex on a daily basis and it's driving her crazy. I guess he's really not her "ex" yet because they are still legally married, but they do live apart. When it comes to the car, financial issues, and their kids, there's a lot of hatred being portrayed by the two of them. Her sons are very angry with their dad and they know how their dad has hurt her. Does it matter if boys or girls are the children that are stuck in the middle? I don't know about girls, but my son seems to be very shielding of me from anyone new that may come into my life. It should be interesting when I do eventually date again.

I guess as the world turns, so does my love life. Well, another idiot down! The third scam artist appeared right on schedule. Are they not comparing notes as to who is scamming whom? This one only took me a couple of hours to bust; I'm quite proud of myself for telling him where to go and go fast. I'm getting really good at catching them in the act of stupidity! When the conversation sounds too good, there's usually a con artist right behind the corner. I'm feeling so empowered now! I'm not letting any man ruin my life, and even though it's Saturday, I've busted three men now who were trying to scam me. But, while taking care of me, I'm also trying to get through to my son. He's hurting inside, but he won't let out his emotions. I need to get through to him, but I don't know how. He needs an outlet, but its nowhere in sight. However, I did schedule a counseling session at my church this evening, and as we all started talking, the results did get underway. He was able to talk to a male role model and get another man's viewpoint on this situation. This associate pastor told my son that it takes two people in a relationship to make or to break up a marriage. Each person is to blame in some way, and sometimes one person breaks those marriage vows in a way that God doesn't agree with. Also, he told him that he needs to be open and honest with his dad in order to get the answers he so desperately needs. They both should talk openly.

This conversation went on for about an hour and by the time it ended, we both had tears in our eyes. I think we both needed to get out of there and just go home. We got into my vehicle, and I handed him a tissue because now the tears were flowing more freely. Even though he was very defiant through this entire conversation, I think it really got to him. Now he had another male who saw this entire time frame of marriage rolled into one hour. He had given my son the advice that he should look at the entire situation instead of blaming his mother for his dad leaving into the arms of another woman. Arriving back home, my son's first reaction was to torment the cat once again. I think he compared my cat with all of the changes I've made in my life and if he irritated the cat, he was in control of at least something in his mom's life. After a brief argument with me, he calmed down and then went to his room. I gave him some time alone and then suggested that he write down his burning questions that he wanted to ask his dad. He was like me, I guess, I did better when I had my notes together and didn't try to think on the fly. My organizational skills were better served when I was prepared. Before I knew it, he was in on the computer asking me how to spell certain words. This took him about 10 minutes, and then he printed them out. I didn't even want to read his list. This was personal to him and something he had to deal with. I hope this is the start of his acceptance of his demons. I am trying to support him through this mess, and I have to be stronger than him. At least those are my thoughts right now. I feel that I am moving forward, but I have found that I am being pulled backwards into his world and into a vat of oil that has boiled my tribulations for years. This makes me angry somewhat—I guess that roller coaster of emotions has resurfaced once again. Will this ever end and will my life and my son's life ever get back on track and go smoothly again?

When my son left this afternoon to his dad's place, those feelings of loneliness were very strong once more. I tried to shove them aside, but they started nudging at me more than normal. This transition time was somewhat harder than the last. I guess I just deserve someone in my life that completes me too. Right? When I was married, I was so into my son and his needs, and I took care of the house the same way. But, my ex never seemed to need the caring and compassion that I wanted to give. So, now, I'm focusing on myself. I'm buying what I had wanted when I was with him, but he said, "No." I'm changing the look of the house as I see fit, and I'm taking into consideration the needs of no one else but me. This is hard to admit, but now that I've done it, it seems like someone has stolen my soul and is acting as if she were a child and doing what they want within me. I now know why my ex enjoyed that comfort. It was all about him and his needs. It's a very gratifying feeling to consider no one but you as number one. Am I being as selfish as he? Perhaps, but do I finally deserve some "me" time? This brings back memories from church this morning that told me that God gives us time to deal with our issues and if we don't, he will make them public. Boy, is this public! He has drug us all through the mud, and I'm sure many more people know about this mess than I realize.

CHAPTER 15

Next Steps

aybe I need a new goal, or a new direction. But, the only thing I do know is that the Bible says God hates divorce, and since we had no way to reconcile since it was his decision to leave permanently, I feel that I have been vindicated. I could never take him back even though I can forgive him. I cannot forget that he has lied and cheated against me, and I cannot tolerate his actions for even a second. I'm sure he sees this situation in a different light than me. In his eyes, I'm sure it's some or even my entire fault that he has chosen his actions.

Each day brings new challenges, but now my ups and downs are getting few and far between, but yesterday was definitely a down day. That solitude crept back once more. It never seems to be very far away from me, because it shows up when I don't need those emotions. Even my friends who are also going through a divorce weigh heavy on my mind. What has become of us? We're like the poster children for bad marriages. Our lives have dramatically changed and there is no one with an instruction booklet to tell us our next step in solving this puzzle.

On a good note, I am proud of Mary for getting stronger, and more self-assured. I'm proud of the progress she's made through this rough patch of hers. She's standing up for herself and her kids. Her ex is still acting like a jerk still, but she's defending her actions and not letting that bastard get to her as much as he once did. His life is the one that is crumbling, but he can't see it and he becomes defensive when she points it out. He's the one who needs counseling even more than her. As for me, my friend Marie has been an integral part of my dilemma. I talk to her everyday and even though she's only a few years older than me, she has been my inspiration. Her words of comfort and advice have really saved me from myself. She has given me hope when there was none to see from afar. I guess God sends angels into your life when you least expect them, and they definitely have their work cut out when it comes to my crumbling life.

Even today I have seen a different side of his adventure. I took my son's book back to him at school since he left it at my house the other day. As I was talking to one of the teachers, she had mentioned that a lady had dropped off my son at school one morning. I told her it was probably my ex's girlfriend. She said that as she was walking into the building she waved to her, because that's what she did—she would wave at the parents to say hello. But, that day there was no response from "her." Was his new chick angry that now she has some more responsibility in her life to raise another man's child? Were things that bad in her life, or was this new relationship going down hill and she didn't know where to turn next? Several more questions entered my mind and they were all negative. I wasn't sure what to think of her actions, but there was one person we all had in common— my son, the victim.

As I look around to the other victims, I see Mary making another step closer to healing her pain. Yesterday, October 1, she stopped wearing her wedding ring. This is a big step for her, and a major decision in her life. I've seen her grow more confident in these last couple of weeks than in the last three months. I think with everyone's support, she will get to that next phase—the "I don't care about him" phase. Undoing another's decision or even coping with divorce is quite an effort for us all, but getting to the point of not caring about "their" life now is even harder than dealing with your own sometimes. However, I know that I have to focus harder than ever before on my own life in order to survive.

My day did go better today though. I met another guy on my dating service, and we had talked a couple of times via e-mail. The strange part was that last night he gave me his phone number and said to call him. Gee, a guy who lives locally and wants me to call him on the phone—not correspond on the Internet? This should be interesting—I'll call him after work tomorrow. Well we did talk, and we found out that we had a lot on common. We both are ex-military, so we had a lot in common in that respect. I even told him I was writing a book and he asked me about it. I was waiting for a negative response, so I hesitantly told him what it was about. I actually got a laugh out of him. So, I haven't scared him off yet. But, we'll see. I'm really going slowly on this one—no more quick relationships for me! I'm beginning to hate this "dating" scene again. I've had so many negative men in my life lately. Can any man really give me the joy I so desperately need? I'm so scared that they are out there just lining up to destroy my heart.

Well, this evening we talked some more. I found out about his past relationships and he about mine. It's interesting that we both have ex's who have cheated on us during our past marriages. The only strange thing about both of us, that is the same, is that we don't have a lot of bitterness about that part of our lives. I mean there's always going to be some regret, some loss and definitely some since of hurt, but we have moved on the next level. Time will only tell if we are compatible. I'm not jumping into something else too fast this time—this on-line dating thing is scary enough.

It's now Sunday morning, and once again I heard another message that touched me greatly. The Pastor, today, spoke of controlling your thought process. This subject really captured my attention for all of the grief I've put up with and all of the divorces happening around me, including my own. He spoke of how memories can continually replay themselves, capture your way of thinking, and then control your every emotion. It's a way of going to a place of remembrance whether it is bad or good. He said that the way to control this is to change your mind by reprogramming the way you think. One's thought pattern needs to be changed, or you will keep reliving the same destructiveness until the hurt has deepened. In addition, single moms and men have a tendency to go to this place due to decisions that they have to make, and they're not sure if the decisions they've made are the correct ones. One must let go of the past in order to move forward. In the end, you can cling to the prize in your future that you so desperately deserve. This was powerful information to digest, and to carry it within me will be a challenge.

The idea that a person can become captive in their life by looking at those things which has emotional control over you, is just no way to live. There seems to be no way to get past these emotions, and one can feel that there is no way to break them down. A suggestion that he made was to be on the offensive— don't let your thought-life attack you. You must tell your thoughts where to go, not the other way around. For if you don't, these thoughts can propel you into another dimension or they can cripple you. Because, how you think everyday affects you. You can either turn yourself around or you can continue in circles. He also stated that how you act affects those around you—just ask them. If they're honest and want to help, they will. This message was so powerful to me that I called Mary to listen to his pod cast. I couldn't get in touch with her, but I know this is the message she needs to hear. I was quite moved by it, and I think I will always remember how it forever changed   my way of thinking.

It's now Monday, and everyone at work wanted to know about my weekend. I told them that I had the best time. I told them that I went out with a true gentleman. His face was real; his personality was unique—he was real—he didn't only exist on the Internet, I actually met him. We had a great time. Boy, I could really get used to this type of treatment. My only problem i s that it's so hard to believe someone could treat me so nice. All of my life I had been so attracted to guys who wanted to be in charge and who didn't respect women. It wasn't apparent at first, but after I had been pulled in, it was too late, and I was stuck. Why? I really don't know, but it was almost impossible to escape after a period of time. Perhaps, it had something to do with my dad who was an alcoholic. I guess the old saying is that you are attracted to what you know—in my case, it was a man who didn't respect himself as well as the people around him. This may be why I am stronger than I realize, because I have felt tragedy in the past and I have survived. I know I can get to the next phase of my life with or without a man beside me.

So, with that in mind, I think any new man in my life will have trouble understanding that it is hard for me to trust again with my whole heart. I work with several ladies who saw me start in my fall from grace, and my ultimate divorce. In between my ups and downs, I know they were all there to protect me and comfort me in my days of sadness. They are here to comfort me—I just know it. Besides, I even got a comment that said that the "Divorce Mafia" would have been all over this guy if he hurt one hair on my head. Now that's what I call friends! I am very thankful for them, for they have made my crisis their own, and they are there for me.

Today is a mile-marker; it's October 6—this day would have marked another anniversary with that man. But instead of getting totally ignored with no present, I sit here at my desk staring at red roses from the new man in my life. It's all a little too much—I've only known him for a week. My ex never did anything like that this soon. It's a little overwhelming, but I like the attention. I don't want my heart to be hurt or broken so soon—AGAIN! I just seem to be a magnet for guys out to break me emotionally.

As for Mary, well, I'm really proud of her once again. Now, she's finally getting some closure that she so desperately needs. She confronted the other woman and got some answers to questions she's had all along. In addition to telling her ex that she had talked to her, he was suddenly dumbfounded. After his silence, she told him what he needed to hear—she wanted him out of her life for good. Boy, that was a giant step for her and I'm really happy that she's gotten this far. My other friend, Jackie, is another case in point. If only she could get on with her love life—she's been divorced for about two years now, and she really hasn't gotten back into the dating game yet. She has been stuck with her ex with his depression and alcoholism problems even after the divorce. She can't even get a break since she has two boys and can't trust her ex with them so she can do anything new in her life. Having her boys all the time, she's the primary parent in their lives and she can't wander too far. She's even having trouble getting involved in a new relationship because of him. This has been one of her concerns for so long, and it's interesting how a divorce presents issues that can't be downplayed. There seems to be at least something about our ex that seems to haunt us and we can never shake it. However, each of us will make it through, but it will take us a lot of time.

This last week has really been interesting. This new guy has really captured my attention. He really seems to care for me; I'm not used to someone who really goes out of their way for me like that. His attentiveness and concern is overwhelming. I don't feel like I totally have to take care of myself. He's there to pick me up when I fall. I don't feel like everything is up to me, and only me, to fix or take care of each day. Wow! Where's this guy been all my life? I didn't think there were any more men like him out there. I was definitely wrong and now I'm trying to just enjoy my time with him. It's been really hard to get used to this type of treatment, but I'm trying to let my feelings show. It will take me time to let my thoughts show and to trust again in a relationship. It will be hard, too, to love again—but I'm willing to try.

Trying to establish a relationship with someone new is a challenge after a divorce, but I still have to deal with my ex since we have a son less than 18 years old and still dependent on both of us. It's even harder when your ex says something stupid like his girlfriend is such a good parent—perhaps even better than both of us combined. Who comes up with his words? I think he needs more counseling! If she's such a good parent, why is she teaching her kids how to commit adultery? My idea of good parent is that you set an example for them to emulate. You don't fool around with a married man or a married woman. I don't think he'll ever get it—I don't think I'll be alive if the time comes when he ever does, because I'd probably be 110 years old by then.

Each day since my divorce, I have re-examined my life in several ways. I have grown emotionally, my life has changed drastically, and I have gained the freedom that I so desperately need. It feels like a dream or sometimes a nightmare. I want so much to get back to what I consider a "normal" life again. But, what is considered normal after a divorce? My son is only with me every other week, I live alone now with animals who can't talk back to me, but try. Is that normal? I'm totally in awe when I wake up to a new day that presents to me issues that I don't want to deal with alone. I'm also afraid to get back into a relationship that seems to be going too quickly. So, what's my advice to myself? I guess proceeding at a steady pace and not taking each moment for granted because life hits you hard sometimes, but I must be strong. I'm getting the help from my friends and family, and perhaps a therapist, but I can't do it alone.

My current love life scares me silly. I have to go slow with this new "project" in my life. I'm fresh out of a two decade marriage, and I am proceeding cautiously and slow is my new goal in life. I don't know how this will end, but I need to just go for it, and see how my life will turn out. I'm still scared, but I need to just try and love again. There will be times where I won't know the answers, but they will come. I just need to learn that all men are not like my ex. I just have to enjoy the ride that gets me to the next stage of my life that has changed for the better. I know now that my ex has given me a gift that I once viewed as a train wreck that ruined my life. But, now I see my life as a challenge and not a stumbling block. My thoughts are now in the pursuit of my future interests. I can't look back on the past for it would devastate me. There are better things to do with my time and wonderful people to meet that will influence my life's path, and for the better. I know now that my prior life was "practice" for my next life. I was used and definitely abused in that relationship, and now I have the independence and willingness to do better with this second chance at life. Remember, it's better to laugh, and not cry, because you spilled the milk and broke the bottle in the process. That milk was probably spoiled in the first place! I am learning to laugh at my troubles and replace those bad thoughts with good ones—life is more pleasant if I can just do this one thing for myself.

The End

www.ingramcontent.com/pod-product-compliance
Lightning Source LLC
Chambersburg PA
CBHW070911120626
46546CB00001B/219